# FOREVER SUMMER

Also by Nigella Lawson

**HOW TO EAT**
THE PLEASURES AND PRINCIPLES OF GOOD FOOD

**HOW TO BE A DOMESTIC GODDESS**
BAKING AND THE ART OF COMFORT COOKING

**NIGELLA BITES**

# FOREVER SUMMER

## NIGELLA LAWSON

PHOTOGRAPHS BY PETRINA TINSLAY

Chatto & Windus
LONDON

First published in 2002

1 3 5 7 9 10 8 6 4 2

First published in the United Kingdom in 2002 by Chatto & Windus
Random House, 20 Vauxhall Bridge Road, London SW1V 2SA

Random House Australia (Pty) Limited
20 Alfred Street, Milsons Point, Sydney, New South Wales 2061, Australia

Random House New Zealand Limited
18 Poland Road, Glenfield, Auckland 10, New Zealand

Random House South Africa (Pty) Limited
Endulini, 5a Jubilee Road, Parktown 2193, South Africa

Random House UK Limited Reg. No. 954009

www.randomhouse.co.uk

A CIP catalogue record for this book is available from the British Library.

ISBN 0 7011 7381 5

Design and Art Direction: Caz Hildebrand
Cookery Assistants: Hettie Potter with Angela Boggiano
Additional research: Skye Gyngell
Stylist: Helen Trent
Index: Vicki Robinson

Papers used by Random House are natural, recyclable products made from wood grown in
sustainable forests. The manufacturing processes conform to the environmental regulations
of the country of origin.

Printed by Appl Druck, Wemding, Germany

# CONTENTS

# INTRODUCTION

In the ideal world inhabited by the chef, there may indeed be a place for the lyrical insistence on using only those ingredients that the month in hand offers up to the market place, but my kitchen, my home, the way I cook, resist such purist strictures. For much as I love the idea of wandering out to the shops, basket dangling from my arm, to gather each new season's freshly ripened produce, I neither have the time to shop that way, nor the discipline – and, frankly, I baulk at such loftily imposed restraints. I shop and cook much as I eat, with greedy opportunism.

Seasonal cooking is anyway better suited to those who live in sunnier climates. The rest of us need to make the most of what warmth is offered, and much of the time this has to emanate from the kitchen rather than from the skies outside. Summer, then, is an idea, a memory, a hopeful projection. Sometimes when it's grey outside and cold within, we need to conjure up the sun, some light, a lazy feeling of having all the wide-skied time in the world to sit back and eat warmly with friends. I am not talking about creating some overblown idyll of perpetual Provençal summer, but of extending that purring sense of sunny expansiveness.

Summer food, even when eaten in deepest winter, contains within it the idea of simple cooking. But the best recipes are never blueprints, only ideas hungrily mooted. The ones in this book have come to me the way they always do, plundered from friends, from family, grown out of an idea of what might go with what. As the Australian food writer Maggie Beer has written, 'cooking is all about osmosis – a mental note made about a flavour combination or a technique, a memory of a dish'. Cooking is not just about applying heat, procedure, method, but about transformation of a more intimate kind; none of us cooks without bringing our own character to bear on the food in front of us. Just as the recipes that follow have been toyed with, changed, fiddled with to become my food, so I expect them to be remodelled in your own kitchen.

I have only one rule when I decide what to put in, what to leave out. However successful a kitchen experiment might seem to be, if I don't feel the urge to cook something again, and soon, I ditch it. The one-off spectacular is not my style, nor ever could be. And, if at any time I'm still wondering if this or that particular recipe is worth keeping, I set myself a scene: a friend, a reader, a fellow-mother at the school gates, is coming up to me, telling me that tonight she's going to cook my …….. If I'm not filled with impatient, evangelical enthusiasm at the imagined exchange, if that recipe doesn't inspire that same, unwavering, bossy confidence, then out it goes. I want to write only about the food I love, and I want you to love it, too.

Life has its difficulties, why add to them in the kitchen? And for all that my title archly conjures up that starlet's gushing hope – from the première scene in *Singing in the Rain* – that 'if I've brought a little cheer into your humdrum little lives, it ain't all been in vain for nothin'', it is not because I believe there is nothing but endless, unclouded blue sky in Nigellaland, but because I still believe the kitchen is not a place you escape from, but the place you escape to.

# CONVERSION CHARTS

## OVEN TEMPERATURES

| gas mark | °C | description |
|---|---|---|
| ½ | 120 | very cool |
| 1 | 140 | |
| 2 | 150 | cool |
| 3 | 160 | warm |
| 4 | 180 | moderate |
| 5 | 190 | fairly hot |
| 6 | 200 | |
| 7 | 210 | hot |
| 8 | 220 | very hot |
| 9 | 240 | |

## Weights

| ounces | grams |
|---|---|
| 1 | 25 |
| 2 | 50 |
| 3 | 75 |
| 4 | 110 |
| 5 | 150 |
| 6 | 175 |
| 7 | 200 |
| 8 | 225 |
| 9 | 250 |
| 10 | 275 |
| 11 | 315 |
| 12 | 350 |
| 13 | 365 |
| 14 | 400 |
| 15 | 425 |
| 16/1lb | 450 |

## Volumes

| fluid ounces | millilitres |
|---|---|
| 1 | 25 |
| 2 | 55 |
| 3 | 75 |
| 4 | 120 |
| 5 | 150 |
| 6 | 175 |
| 7 | 200 |
| 8 | 225 |
| 9 | 250 |
| 10 | 275 |
| 15 | 425 |
| 20/1 pint | 570 |
| $1\frac{1}{4}$ pints | 725 |
| $1\frac{1}{2}$ pints | 850 |
| $1\frac{3}{4}$ pints | 1 litre |

# FIRST COURSE

# CROSTINI DEL MARE

I've been harbouring a memory of these for eight years now, but this is the first time I've actually cooked them myself. I came across them while I was on holiday in Porto Ercole, at a little restaurant called Il Greco over the way in Porto Santo Stefano. I sat by the water's edge, voluptuously savouring the menu while the waiters brought plates of lozenge-shaped toasts covered with the still warm meat of finely chopped mussels and clams, deep with garlic and sprinkled with parsley. It was when I was cooking the pasta with mussels for the book shoot that the briney, winey smell of the steaming seafood made me desperate to recreate these. And yes, they're fiddly, but so very, very good.

You will have a little pool of marine juices left after you've chopped and smeared the seafood for the crostini and the best way I can think of for using this up is to dunk the remaining half of your French loaf straight into it and slurp it all up. You can of course, though, just bag it up as it is and freeze it so you have a small but concentrated stash of deep-scented fish stock to use at some later date. And once you get into the habit of crostini-production (and I find I do), you might find it easier anyway to buy a baguette, or ficelle (either will do), slice it and bag it up and keep it in the deep-freeze to be oil-dabbled and toasted whenever you want.

| | |
|---|---|
| **Half a skinny baguette** | **2 tablespoons olive oil** |
| **(in other words, a ficelle)** | **750g mussels** |
| **approx. 4 tablespoons olive oil** | **500g clams** |
| **2 cloves garlic minced** | **1 tablespoon vermouth or white wine** |
| **2 tablespoons finely chopped parsley,** | |
| **plus more to decorate** | |

Preheat the oven to 200°C/gas mark 6. Cut the bread into slices, about half to three-quarters of a centimetre thick: in other words, neither too thick, nor too thin. You need about 25 slices for the amount of chopped seafood topping here. Using a pastry brush or your fingers, dab the bread, on both sides, with the olive oil and sit these lightly oil-brushed slices on a rack over a roasting tin and bake for about 5–10 minutes, turning once. Frankly, it's just a matter of cooking until the slices begin to turn gold, and this takes more time the fresher the bread. In other words, if you've got stale bread, use it for this. When the bread is toasted and gold, remove it from the oven and leave it to cool while you get on with the mussels and clams.

Put the garlic and parsley into a large saucepan with the oil and cook, stirring, over a low heat for a couple of minutes making sure it doesn't colour. Tip in the cleaned mussels and clams, turn the heat to high, add the tablespoon of vermouth or wine and clamp on the lid. Cook for 4–5 minutes, shaking the pan a few times to disperse the shells until they are all gaping open. Remove the lid and take off the heat so that the shellfish can cool a little, then pick out the meat with your fingers.

Chop the shellfish flesh finely with a mezzaluna or knife (you can use the processor but be careful not to turn everything into undifferentiated mush), then spread on to the crostini and sprinkle over some more chopped parsley. Eat while still warm.

Makes approx. 25.

# GRIDDLED AUBERGINES WITH FETA, MINT AND CHILLI

You can griddle these aubergines, grill them or just blitz them in the heat of the barbecue: I really don't care. The point is this: once your slices of aubergine are cooked, you pile up one short end with lemon-soused crumbled feta, chopped red chilli and fresh mint and roll the whole thing up; it's really more of an assembly job than cooking.

I tend to think of these simple involtini as an ideal vegetable picky-thing to serve either as a starter before, or alongside, a generally meat-heavy barbecue, but they don't have to be: frankly, just serve these with drinks and you don't have to think of a first course for the rest of summer. And I eat these happily deep into winter too.

2 large aubergines, each cut thinly, lengthwise, into about 10 slices
4 tablespoons olive oil
250g feta cheese
1 large red chilli, finely chopped, deseeded or not, depending on how much heat you want

large bunch fresh mint, finely chopped, with some saved for sprinkling over at the end
juice of 1 lemon
black pepper

Preheat the barbecue or griddle to a high heat.

Brush both sides of the aubergine slices with the oil, and cook them for about 2 minutes each side until golden and tender.

Crumble the feta into a bowl and stir in the chilli, mint and lemon juice and grind in some black pepper. You don't need salt, as the feta is salty enough. Pile the end third of each warm aubergine slice with a heaped teaspoon of the feta mixture and roll each slice up as you go to form a soft, stuffed bundle.

Place join side down on a plate, and sprinkle with a little more mint.

Makes 20 rolls.

# HOT SALT COD FRITTERS WITH COLD SEAFOOD SALAD

These are actually two completely independent, separate recipes, but I so love the palate-searing, heavy hotness of the potato-fluffy fritters with the anise-clear coolness of the seafood salad that I had, quite bossily, to stick them together here.

## SEAFOOD SALAD

Feel free to alter the relative amounts of seafood in this; indeed, play with it as you want to. Don't think of making it just for some planned-for, guest-invited meal, though: nothing's lovelier, in the summer (and beyond), than to have a huge, cold bowlful of this, standing in the fridge, for you to pick from when you want.

1 bottle white wine
4 bay leaves
8 black peppercorns
500g baby octopus
500g baby squid, sliced but tentacles left whole
500g medium raw prawns

125ml olive oil
juice of 2 lemons
2 red chillies, deseeded and finely chopped
3 sticks celery, finely sliced
large bunch fresh flat-leaf parsley, chopped
salt, if necessary

Make a stock to cook the seafood in by boiling the wine, bay leaves and peppercorns in a large saucepan.

Cook the octopus, squid and prawns separately in the stock as they will take different times to cook. It's very hard to be specific about lengths of time, though; fish changes in density, relative tenderness and size, from catch to catch. But taste as you go, and fish them out with a slotted spoon as they are done, letting them cool in a bowl. The liquid will go quite murky but that's to be expected, so don't be alarmed.

Whisk together the oil and lemon juice, and add the finely chopped chillies. Pour this mixture over the cooled seafood and add the celery and chopped parsley, mixing everything together thoroughly. Check the seasoning and add salt if necessary. Add enough of the cooled stock to cover the salad so that it macerates completely covered in juice.

Keep in the fridge and let the flavours develop for at least a couple of hours; after a day, this will really come into its own, though. Spoon out excess liquid, if there is any, drizzle over a little more olive oil if you like, and sprinkle over a bit more chopped parsley.

Serves 6–8.

# SALT COD FRITTERS

I can't pretend these aren't fiddly to make, but they aren't hard. The most taxing thing really is that you have to remember to start soaking the salt cod 24 hours before you want to cook it, and you do have to change the water regularly (just pour out then replace the water every time you think of it, or about four times during the whole soaking period). A friend of mine once told me that the best way of soaking salt cod was by sitting it in the lavatory cistern, so that everytime someone flushes you get a change of water. I wanted to try this but the protestations in my household when I suggested it, were simply not worth putting up with. I can't quite see the problem, though, since you're hardly soaking the fish in the water from the lavatory bowl, but the fresh water kept in the cistern. Still, perhaps you'll have more luck.

**500g salt cod, soaked for 24 hours, changing the water regularly**
**500g maincrop potatoes, peeled and quartered**
**600ml milk**
**2 bay leaves**
**1 egg, beaten**

**4 tablespoons chopped fresh parsley**
**quarter onion, finely grated, to give about 2 tablespoons**
**1 clove garlic, finely grated**
**black pepper**
**sunflower oil for frying**

Drain the salt cod and put it in a saucepan with the potatoes, covering both with the milk. Add the bay leaves and bring to the boil, cooking everything for 8–10 minutes, or until the salt cod's tender, then lift it out. Let the potatoes cook for a further 20 minutes.

Let the cod cool slightly, until you can remove any bones without burning your fingers, then flake the fish into a bowl and beat it to threads with a fork or whisk, or even easier still, with the paddle attachment of a free-standing mixer. Drain the potatoes and add them to the fish, mashing them with the beater again. Or you can just push both through the coarse disc of a food mill.

Stir in the beaten egg, chopped parsley, grated onion, garlic and black pepper, adding a little of the poaching liquid to make a smooth mixture. Then shape, using two spoons, into quenelles or lozengey forms. Place these on baking sheets, lined with cling-film (so they don't stick), and sit them in the fridge to cool completely before you fry them. This helps them hold their shape.

Heat some oil in a frying pan to make a layer of about 1cm, and drop in the fritters a few at a time. Cook, turning as necessary, until golden on all sides, and drain on kitchen paper.

Makes about 20.

Given that I made this out of my head rather than out of a book, I don't know how authentically Thai it is, but I do know it's authentically wonderful. What I was after was that first course (among many) I always order in Thai restaurants, of crumbled meat, quite dry, sour-sharp with chilli, which you eat by scooping with crunchy, boat-shaped lettuce leaves.

One of the joys of this, in my version at any rate, is how easy and quick it is to make. If you're having people over to dinner midweek, you could make this as a first course before a plain roast chicken and provide a full-on dinner with next to no effort. Mind you, as a meal in its entirety, for three or four of you, it takes some beating, too. Reduce quantities (or not) for a five-minute supper for one.

You may need to be rather brutal with the lettuce as you tear the leaves off to provide the edible wrappers for the beef, which is why I specify one to two icebergs. If you want to perk the leaves up a little, making sure they curve into appropriate repositories for later, leave them in a sinkful of very cold water while you cook the minced beef, then make sure you drain them well before piling them up on their plate.

| | |
|---|---|
| 1 teaspoon vegetable oil | zest and juice of 1 lime |
| 2 red birdeye chillies, finely chopped | 3–4 tablespoons chopped fresh |
| 375g beef mince | coriander |
| scant tablespoon Thai fish sauce | 1–2 iceberg lettuces |
| 4 spring onions, dark green bits removed, | |
| finely chopped | |

Put the oil in a non-stick frying pan on medium heat and when warm add the finely chopped chillies and cook for a couple of minutes, stirring occasionally. It's wiser not to leave the pan, as you don't want them to burn. Add the beef, turn up the heat and, breaking up the mince with a wooden spoon or fork, cook for 3 or 4 minutes till no trace of pink remains. Add the fish sauce and, still stirring, cook till the liquid's evaporated. Off the heat, stir in the spring onions, zest and juice of the lime and most of the coriander. Turn into a bowl, and sprinkle over the remaining coriander just before serving.

Arrange the iceberg lettuce leaves on another plate – they should sit one on top of another easily enough – and let people indulge in a little DIY at the table, filling cold crisp leaves with spoonfuls of sharp, spicy, hot, crumbled meat.

Serves 6.

# RICE PAPER ROLLS

I'll be honest with you: I had longed to make some version of these little rolls for years but either essential laziness or fear that they would be frighteningly complicated put me off. Now that I've made them, I can't quite see what I was on about. Fiddly they may be, but I think they must be one of the easiest recipes to make in the whole book. And also one of the loveliest: there is something about the light, unwheatenness of rice pasta (which in effect these sheets just are) and the bundles of fresh herbs within that make them compulsive and uplifting eating. You can, and this is how I ate them first in a Vietnamese restaurant, add some cooked prawns and cooled, stir-fried chopped pork along with the herbs and rice vermicelli, but I can't honestly see that you need to.

You can often find the rice pancakes, or rice sheets (emphatically not rice paper) in the supermarket. If you're unlucky in this respect, you will have to track down an Asian store, which offers a gastro-reward of its own.

| | |
|---|---|
| **100g rice vermicelli** | **bunch fresh Thai basil, roughly chopped** |
| **1 tablespoon rice vinegar** | **half a cucumber, cut into thin batons** |
| **1 tablespoon soy sauce** | **6 spring onions, finely sliced** |
| **1 tablespoon Thai fish sauce** | **12 rice pancakes** |
| **bunch fresh mint, roughly chopped** | **soy sauce for serving (optional)** |

Soak the vermicelli according to the instructions on the packet, and drain once the translucent threads are rehydrated.

Flavour the vermicelli with the rice vinegar, soy and fish sauces, and then add the chopped herbs, cucumber and spring onions. Mix gently with your hands to try to combine the noodles, herbs and vegetables.

Soak the rice pancakes (again, according to packet instructions) in a shallow bowl of hot water and then lay each one on a tea towel to pat dry. Run a fairly narrow strip of noodle mixture down the middle of the pancake, fold over one half and then carefully roll it up as tightly as you can. Slice each roll into four and then arrange them on a plate.

If you want, pour some soy sauce into a few little bowls for dipping the rolls into as you eat. They are also fabulous with the Vietnamese dipping sauce, in the form of the dressing on page 75.

Makes 48 rolls.

# GINGER-CURED SALMON

I know that suggesting you cure anything sounds as if I am about to get you in a mob cap sitting in a pantry for days on end, but just think marinade: the ingredients and the fridge do all the work. And look at it this way: the steeping, which asks very little of you in the first place, means you then dispense with any actual cooking later.

I suppose this is a tentatively Asian gravadlax, but I think it's important not to get bogged down in post-hoc definitions. All you need to know is that you end up with fleshy salmon, salty-sweet and infused with the hot breath of ginger, edged aromatically with a grassy green covering of coriander. Eat it finely sliced as it is for a starter, or with a salad and maybe some steamed new potatoes as a light lunch.

1kg salmon fillet, skinned, pin boned and of equal thickness throughout its length

50g fresh ginger, coarsely microplaned (or otherwise minced or grated)

4 tablespoons Maldon salt

4 tablespoons caster sugar

juice of 2 limes

bunch fresh coriander, chopped

Put the salmon into a dish large enough for the fillet to lie flat, skinned side down. Combine the ginger, salt, sugar and lime juice and press it on to the top of the salmon, spreading evenly. Sprinkle over the chopped coriander so that there is a thick layer of dark leafy green.

Cover the dish with clingfilm, weigh the fish down – I just sit three or so unopened cans of tomatoes on top of the clingfilm – and stick it in the fridge for three to five days.

When you want to eat it, just remove your weights and the clingfilm, transfer the lawn-bordered piece of fish to a wooden board and slice across at an angle as thinly as you can manage.

Serves 6–8.

# BABY OCTOPUS AND POTATO SALAD

You really need the teensy weensy, almost miniature-sized baby octopus for this, which means you need a fishmonger, and a good one at that, to prepare this. Failing that, just alter the focus a little and buy squid – grown-up ones – and chop them into 3cm slices, cook them for about half the time of the octopus and add a few peas along with the potatoes at the end. But if you can get baby octopus, count yourself fortunate. I love the tender, warm graininess of this; the way the garlicky, chilli, mellow seafood juices ooze their way into the potato. For this reason I use maincrop potatoes, and peel them, but by all means cube waxier-fleshed new potatoes if you are not as greedily keen as I am on all that floury absorbency.

I've stipulated marinating the octopus for an hour, but to be honest, the longer the better. A day in the fridge will do it no harm whatsoever.

6 tablespoons olive oil

juice of 2 lemons

2 cloves garlic

1 long red fresh chilli

750g baby octopus

2 large potatoes (approximately 750g total weight), peeled

salt

small bunch fresh parsley, chopped

Get out a dish or, easier, a large freezer bag, and pour in the olive oil, squeeze in the lemon juice, mince in the garlic and deseed and finely chop the chilli and bung that in too. Add the octopus, tie up the bag and squelch so that the octopus gets turned in the marinade, then leave it to steep for at least an hour. Unless you're giving it a day or so, and it's not too hot, it's better to let it marinate out of the fridge.

Cut the peeled potatoes into rough 2cm cubes and boil them in salted water until tender. Heat a wide, heavy-bottomed pan, and tip the octopus into it. Fry for about 5 minutes to colour the octopus a little, pushing them around in the pan as you do so, but don't worry about adding any more oil at this stage as there will be enough clinging to them from the marinade. Turn the heat down, scrape in what remains of the marinade, then cover the pan and cook slowly until the octopus is beginning to become tender, which will take about 45 minutes though you could optimistically check after 30 minutes. Then add the potatoes and continue cooking, for another 10 minutes or so, by which time the octopus should be soft and tender and the potatoes blurry around the edges and fused flavoursomely into the whole, but not actually disintegrating. Turn into a dish, sprinkle with chopped parsley and leave to get to room temperature before eating.

Serves 4–6.

I don't mean to mislead you with the term pizza: I mean to evoke more the style, the way of eating these, than to invoke the Italian original. I have to say, I also love proper pizza cooked this way, on the barbecue, but in high summer, making up batches of yeasted dough can seem uninviting at the very least. Besides, while shopbought flatbreads are fabulous, prepackaged pizza bases most definitely are not.

These vaguely Eastern Mediterranean versions of pizza are perfect for adding to a full-flown barbecue or to cook in a very hot oven or under a blistering grill to go with drinks any time.

The flatbreads I use here are labelled 'white bread khobez' but I don't see why you can't substitute any flatbreads you can lay your hands on. Za'atar – or zhatar – is a highly seasoned spice mixture of dried thyme, sumac and sesame (see my Za'atar Chicken with Fattoush recipe on page 134); halloumi is a hard Greek cheese, squeaky and salty, like edible polystyrene, which is the only way I know how to describe it, and wholly addictive: both are commonly available in supermarkets. These three suggested toppings are merely a start: the method lends itself pretty much to whatever elaboration you like.

I tend to cut these flatbread pizzas into spindly wedges, but leaving them whole is also an option; whatever, they're best eaten hot straight off the barbecue as they tend to dry out and go splintery once they're cold, but I'm also aware that this admonition is likely to be an unnecessary one.

**for the za'atar flatbread:**

| | |
|---|---|
| **1 tablespoon of za'atar** | **1 flatbread** |
| **1 tablespoon olive oil** | |

Mix the spice in the oil, and pour it over the flatbread. Place on a sheet of foil and cook for 2–3 minutes on a hot, preferably lidded, barbecue, in the hot oven or under the grill.

**for the halloumi and tomato flatbread:**

| | |
|---|---|
| **3 tomatoes, deseeded, roughly chopped** | **half a teaspoon dried mint** |
| **1 flatbread** | **drizzle olive oil** |
| **50g halloumi cheese coarsely crumbled or grated** | **small handful fresh mint** |

Spread the tomatoes over the flatbread (again, placed on a foil sheet) and crumble or grate the halloumi over the top. Sprinkle over the dried mint, drizzle with oil and place on the barbecue (or again, cook in a hot oven or grill). Roughly tear the fresh mint and scatter over the hot bread.

**for the chilli and coriander flatbread:**

1 flatbread

half a teaspoon ground coriander

1 long red chilli, deseeded and finely
  chopped

1 tablespoon olive oil

small handful fresh coriander, chopped

Place the flatbread on a sheet of foil. Mix the ground coriander and chopped chilli in the oil and spread it over the bread, dibbling and spreading it with your fingers. Cook as above, and once it's had its couple of minutes and is blistering hot, remove to a plate – or just to your hands – and sprinkle over the fresh coriander.

# SQUID SALAD WITH LIME, CORIANDER, MINT AND MIZUNA

OK. First off, don't worry if the word mizuna means nothing to you. It's a tenderly peppery Japanese salad leaf, which some greengrocers, and even supermarkets, stock these days, but you can easily use rocket instead.

This is rather different from the seafood salad on page 8: the tender, pink-tinged baby squid are quickly fried, and then coated in a pungent dressing made simply by puréeing a peeled lime along with some coriander, mint, fish sauce, garlic and sugar in the processor. It makes a wonderful starter to a full-blown summer dinner party, but I love it, with nothing before or after, except perhaps a bit of fruit, when I've got a couple of friends coming over for lunch.

**500g baby squid (cleaned weight), cut into rings**
**2–3 tablespoons groundnut oil for frying**
**salt**

*for the dressing:*
**1 (approx. 125g) bunch fresh coriander or mint, or a mixture of both**
**1 clove garlic, peeled**

**1–2 tablespoons fish sauce**
**half a teaspoon caster sugar**
**1 green finger chilli, deseeded (optional)**
**1 lime**
**6 tablespoons groundnut oil**

*for the salad:*
**200g mizuna (or rocket) leaves**
**1 small red onion**

Tear the coriander and mint leaves from the stalks, not worrying if a few stalky bits are attached and throw into the food processor along with the garlic, fish sauce and sugar, plus the chilli if you are using it; this is completely up to you and simply depends on whether you want any heat or not. Peel the lime by first cutting off a slice at the ends so that you can make the lime sit on a wooden board and then just cut strips downwards so that peel, and pith, come off cleanly. Add the peeled lime, halved and with the pips removed, to the bowl and process everything until it is a smooth pulp, then drizzle the oil in, down the funnel, with the motor running, to emulsify the sauce. Scrape into a bowl to use later.

Arrange the salad leaves – mizuna or rocket, whichever you're using – in a bowl or on a large plate. Peel the onion, cut it in half and then slice into very thin half moons and sprinkle them over the greenery.

Slice the baby squid, leaving the tentacles whole, and fry in a large pan with a little groundnut oil; you will have to do this in a couple of batches. Remove the cooked squid to a bowl, sprinkle with salt, then, once you've got all cooked and cooled a little, toss in the lime and herb dressing and arrange over the waiting leaves and onions.

Serves 6.

# SOUPS

Chilled soups have more going for them than mere retro charm. Temperature-cooling, unfussy, as soothing for the cook as the eater, they make the perfect, light summer starter. The pink in this particular soup comes from beetroot, toned down with soured cream and further harmoniously soured by lime; the spices are ground cumin and coriander; the final, velvety emulsion is the purest puce. You don't have to serve this, jugs alongside one another, with the pea and mint soup that follows, but the combination, a glowering take on fifties rose-and-eau-de-nil, is irresistible.

I agree that making vats of stock may not be quite the thing when having to cook for a large number of people in high summer, but believe me I am not suggesting you do any such thing. A good make of fresh chicken stock in a tub will do fine here, as would Benedicta's Touch of Taste chicken bouillon concentrate or Marigold vegetable stock powder. The idea is anyway not to get you slaving over a hot stove right now. You know that song, Summertime, and the cooking is easy...

OK yes, beetroot takes a long time to roast properly, but they taste so good when intensified thus by the oven (not that you have to do anything to them while they cook), and that's the extent of the cooking thereafter. In other words, this is a low-effort enterprise.

| | |
|---|---|
| **2 large or 3 medium raw beetroot** | **1.5 litres hot chicken or vegetable stock** |
| **juice of 1 lime** | **salt and pepper** |
| **1 teaspoon ground cumin** | **2 spring onions, halved lengthwise** |
| **1 teaspoon ground coriander** | **250ml sour cream** |

Preheat the oven to 200°C/gas mark 6. Wrap each beetroot in tin foil and bake for one and a half to two hours until tender. Unwrap partly and leave for a while until bearable to touch. And I'd put on washing up gloves for this, too, or you'll have a touch of the Lady Macbeth's about you after. Gingerly peel them – when they're this well cooked the skin should rub off easily – and then cut them into chunks. Put them in the processor with the juice of the lime, the cumin and coriander and blitz to a pulp while pouring the stock down the funnel. You may want to wear an apron for this (or stand well back). Indeed, you may feel happier doing this in two batches. Taste for salt and pepper, blitz again and then pour into a large jug. Add the split spring onions and leave to cool before chilling, clingfilmed, in the fridge for up to three days.

Just before you want to eat this, pick out the spring onions and, to make for a desirably creamy base, blitz again while adding the sour cream (175ml first, then see if you want the rest). Decant back into the jug (for easier pouring) then duly pour into waiting teacups. If you're using more capacious soup bowls in place of the cups, you may find you feed only six from this.

Serves 6–8.

# CHILLED PEA AND MINT SOUP

This is such a lovely, fresh and soothing emulsion, that I am happy to keep a jug of it, for a solo-supper or between-meal refuelling, in the fridge at any time in summer. And while I quite see the sense in using new sugar-sweet peas while they're about, most peas lounge about in shops quite long enough for their pearly sweetness to turn to starch, in which case you can use frozen peas without feeling you're utterly devoid of the seasonal virtues. If you are, however, using fresh peas, drop the pods into the water at the steeping stage, and then boil it all up again for ten minutes, just to extract every last bit of flavour. It'll mean you have to strain the liquid before adding it to the peas themselves, which isn't exactly hard work, but, on top of the podding itself (though children seem to do this gladly, especially if watching TV at the same time) is still another procedure, should such factors hold any weight with you, as they often do with me.

Again, although I've stipulated vegetable stock, I mean nothing more troublesome than adding a tablespoon or so of Benedicta's Touch of Taste vegetable bouillon concentrate or Marigold vegetable stock powder to water.

**1.25 litres vegetable stock**
**stalks from a bunch fresh mint with the**
   **leaves saved**
**1 tablespoon dried mint**
**500g frozen petits pois (or 1.5 kilos of**
   **fresh peas, podded, pods reserved)**

**2 tablespoons olive oil**
**3 spring onions, finely chopped**
**salt and pepper**
**1 x 284ml carton sour cream**

Pour the stock into a large jug or pan and add the fresh mint stalks and the dried mint and leave to steep for 20 minutes to half an hour. If you're using fresh peas, pour the stock directly into a pan along with the mints and pods and boil for about 10–15 minutes and then strain into a jug.

Pour the oil into a large saucepan and warm over medium heat. Add the chopped spring onions and turn in the warm oil for a few minutes until slightly softened, but certainly not caught in any way and then tumble in the peas. If you're using frozen ones, there is no need to defrost them first.

Cook these, stirring with a wooden spatula all the while, over a low to medium heat until the peas have softened a little. Fish out the mint stalks from the stock and pour into the pan, or use the strained pod stock. It's impossible, really, to say exactly how long it will take for the peas to be sufficiently soft, but think around 20 minutes. Leave to cool, and then blitz, in batches, in a blender or processor. Season to taste. If you're making this at all in advance, it's best to keep the pea purée creamless in the fridge until serving, at which time you should ideally blend it again with the sour cream.

Pour into cups or bowls and sprinkle with the chopped, reserved mint leaves.

Serves 6–8, depending on whether you're using cups or bowls.

# RISI E BISI

This most Venetian of Venetian dishes, of the new season's peas and rice, is somewhere between a soup and risotto. Traditionally, it is served for the first time each year, and ceremonially so, on April 25th. It's actually part of Venetian history: on that day, St Mark's Day, the Doge was given a dish of this prepared from the first new, sugar-sweet peas of the year. To tell the truth, at the risk of repeating myself, unless you are using the youngest, freshest, flower-fragrant peas possible then you might as well just use frozen. Once a pea has sat on a shelf and begun turning to starch, then its supposed freshness – and thus its edge – has gone.

If you have got the fresh peas, then you need to make a stock by simmering the pods for an hour or so (or until very tender) in some water in which you've also added salt, a stick of celery, a bay leaf and some sprigs of parsley. Strain this broth, measure out 1 litre, and push the cooked pods through a food mill back into the liquid.

**1.5 litres water to make pea-stock (see above) or 1.5 litres hot chicken stock or vegetable stock (Marigold stock powder is all right)**

**1 kg fresh peas or 350g frozen petits pois, thawed**

**60g unsalted butter (30g if using fresh peas)**

**5 tablespoons freshly grated parmesan, plus more for serving**

**2 tablespoons olive oil (not extra virgin)**

**1 small onion, very finely chopped**

**3 tablespoons fresh chopped flat-leaf parsley**

**225g risotto rice, preferably Vialone or Carnaroli**

**salt and pepper**

If you're using frozen petits pois, put 15g butter in a small pan and over a gentle heat, sauté 100g of them until tender. Put in the processor, with another 15g butter and a tablespoon of parmesan and blitz to a purée.

In a heavy-bottomed wide saucepan, melt 30g butter together with the oil and gently cook the onion in it. After a couple of minutes add a tablespoon of the parsley and cook, still stirring, for another 3 or so minutes until the onion is beginning to soften. Add either the podded peas or the rest of the thawed frozen petits pois and turn in the buttery onion. Then stir in the rice until the grains are coated and fat-slicked, just as you would when starting off a risotto. But here's the easy part: rather than adding the stock slowly and stirring all the while, with risi e bisi, you add all the stock at once. Stir everything together, add the petits pois purée, cover and leave to simmer for about 15 minutes or until the rice is cooked. Pour into a large warmed bowl, and stir in the remaining parmesan and sprinkle over the parsley. Season to taste. If you want to add a slightly Anglo-edge (utterly desirable here), add some chopped fresh mint along with the parsley. Eat out of shallow soup bowls.

Serves 4.

It may seem surprising to suggest such a thick, substantial soup as a summer basic, but you won't think so once you've tasted it. The sweetness of new potatoes, fresh peas, broad beans, the grassy herbalness of asparagus and then the uncompromisingly radiant sunniness of the basil, which is pounded or processed into a pine-nut-less pesto to drizzle over it all at the end, make you almost want to skip with summeriness. Frankly, this has all the comforting life-salving properties of a winter soup, without the bad weather. How bad can that be?

You know, I hope, that as ever I not only permit but invite the use of good stock concentrate rather than any actual carcass-boiling, and frozen in place of fresh pulses, should that make life easier. Actually it does in one major respect: you do need the broad beans to be shelled as well as podded, and this is easiest to do if you use frozen ones, which you've left to thaw. The skins can be just pinched away, leaving the tender, hyper-coloured greenness of the beans within to pop out without any trouble. If you want, you can add a handful or so of orzo pasta (so called because it resembles barley) or any other small soup pasta you like, ten to twelve minutes before the end of cooking, and this certainly makes the soup more filling as a supper in itself. But what isn't optional is the temperature at which you serve it: this should be scarcely warm still. Tepid isn't a word that buzzes with attractive, flavoursome connotations, but believe me, this is the way you want it.

You do need to stir a good bit of the pesto into the soup in the pan, before ladling it into bowls. I dollop some in and then pour the rest into a bowl for people to drizzle over for themselves as they eat. A block of parmesan and a grater on the table alongside are also necessary.

And it's worth mentioning here that this pesto is wonderful, too, drizzled over cool, white, sliced mozzarella – that buffalo mozzarella that can scarcely seem to contain its milkiness – or indeed used as a dressing for a tomato and mozzarella salad.

**2 tablespoons olive oil**

**1 onion, finely chopped**

**2 cloves garlic, minced**

**2 sticks celery, finely chopped**

**250g new potatoes, quartered**

**2 litres chicken or vegetable stock**

**150g fine green beans, topped, tailed and halved**

**150g baby asparagus, halved lengthwise, or larger asparagus cut into approx. 5cm lengths**

**1kg broad beans, podded and shelled, or 150g frozen**

**300g fresh peas, podded, or 100g frozen petits pois**

**3 courgettes, cut into small cubes**

**150g orzo pasta (optional)**

**salt**

**for the pesto:**
2 cloves garlic

100g fresh basil, stalks removed

50g parmesan, freshly grated, plus more
  for serving

100ml olive oil

In a large wide saucepan, heat the oil and cook the onion, garlic, celery and potatoes together gently for about 10 minutes.

Add the stock to the pan and bring to the boil, then simmer for about 5 minutes before adding the green beans, asparagus, broad beans, peas and courgettes.

Bring the soup back to the boil and simmer until all the vegetables are cooked through, about 20 minutes. It's around this time that you could add the pasta, though you could also put some salted water on to boil, and then cook the pasta in it and drain before adding to the vegetable-nubbly soup.

Meanwhile, to make the basil pesto, either use a pestle and mortar or a food processor. First combine all the ingredients except for the oil, bashing or blitzing, and then slowly drip in the oil, until you have a thick green oily emulsion.

Stir a tablespoon or so of the pesto through the soup, and then ladle into bowls, dolloping a teaspoonful more of the pesto into each bowlful, green on green, as you hand it out.

Serves 6–8.

Forgive the tweeness of the title, but this is a soup of such sunny, mood-enhancing yellowness that it overcomes even the most pervasively innate cynicism. To eat this is to feel cheered; even cooking it gives me a lift. It's incredibly easy to make, but that's not the clincher. This golden broth, rice-thickened and studded with a confetti dice of yellow courgettes and sprightly with lemon is pure joy. You only have to see it to believe it. And not surprisingly in some Middle-Eastern cultures, it is believed, in Claudia Roden's words, that 'eating yellow foods will result in laughter and happiness'. This, then, is a yellow soup to banish the blues.

**500g yellow courgettes (2 large)**
**zest and juice of 1 lemon**
**3 tablespoons olive oil**
**1 teaspoon turmeric**

**1 litre chicken stock**
**100g basmati rice**
**Maldon salt and pepper**

Cut the courgettes – wash them by all means if you want, but don't bother to peel them – into 5mm rings, and then finely dice them. Put them into a pan with the lemon zest and oil, stir to coat, then cook on a gentle heat for about 5 minutes, stirring occasionally, until they've slightly softened.

Stir in the turmeric and pour in the stock and lemon juice and then drop in the rice. And for the stock here, as usual I make up some bouillon concentrate with water; you could use vegetable stock if you prefer, but I love the mellow goldenness you get from chicken. Cook, uncovered, for 10–20 minutes, or just until the courgettes and rice are tender. Taste for seasoning. Leave to cool slightly before serving so that you eat the soup warm rather than hot.

Serves 4–6.

And I sometimes exploit all this marvellous yellowness by making, if this doesn't sound too poncey, a carpaccio of zucchini gialli, yellow courgettes. Just use a vegetable peeler to shave off thin curling strips. You will probably have to lose the central seedy core, so I'd reckon on using about one courgette per person. Just lay the strips of courgette (and see them thus adorning the quail on page 147) on a plate, spritz with lemon and a tiny drizzle of oil, a sprinkle of Maldon salt and feather, if you wish, with a few frondy straggles of fresh dill.

PASTA

# PAPPARDELLE WITH COURGETTES, SULTANAS AND PINE NUTS

If there seems to be a rather small amount of pasta specified for four people here, it's not because I'm exercising portion control, but because egg pappardelle swell voluptuously when cooked and a modest tangle of these dried yellow, wide-cut ribbons will plump up to take, appetite-satisfyingly, the whole panful of slow-cooked, sweet and mushy courgette sauce.

Please don't hesitate about the addition of sultanas: this Moorish touch – the sauce emanates, in essence if not exactly, from Sicily and more generally from the Italian south – is not a fanciful one.

I can't claim that this is a beautiful-looking sauce – the khaki tinge of the slow-cooked courgettes doesn't speak of sprightly summer freshness – but its musky, herbal depth is fabulous enough. Eat on balmy evenings outside, with a bottle of resiny yellow wine, or to give the feeling of the same during a long, cold brutal northern winter. This is comfort food, southern-style.

**15g butter**
**1 tablespoon olive oil**
**750g (4 medium) courgettes**
**1 clove garlic, minced**
**salt and pepper**
**2–3 tablespoons Marsala**

**50g sultanas**
**25g pine nuts**
**250g egg pappardelle**
**3 tablespoons freshly grated parmesan**
**small bunch fresh parsley, chopped**

Heat the butter and oil in a heavy-based saucepan, and cut the courgettes into very fine rounds before adding them to the pan. Mince in the garlic and season with salt and pepper. Cook over a low to medium heat for about 45 minutes, stirring every now and again. When they are ready the courgettes will have sweated down – if you'll forgive the expression – but still retain some colour and shape. In other words, you're looking for a certain mushiness without going so far as out-and-out pulp. Not that it matters: if you forget these are on the stove and let them cook until they reach the state of pure, undifferentiated sauce, you will still have something pretty heavenly on your hands. Besides, in Sicily, you will find that different cooks have different preferences: as ever, there is no one way to cook the same thing.

While all this is going on, warm the Marsala, pour it over the sultanas and leave them to plump up for about 15 minutes, or longer if you want. Once the courgettes are cooked, stir the sultanas and their amber juices into them. Taste for seasoning. Toast the pine nuts by cooking them in a dry frying pan until they turn a golden brown, and remove to a cold plate.

Cook the pasta according to packet instructions, then drain and tip into a warmed bowl. Add the courgette mixture and fold and toss to combine. Sprinkle over the pine nuts, parmesan and most of the chopped parsley and toss everything gently together again. Sprinkle with the remaining parsley and take to the table.

Serves 6 as a starter; 4 as a main course.

## TAGLIOLINI AL PESTO AMARO

This 'bitter pesto' is not alarmingly so, but the rocket certainly gives a more rasping bite than the softer herbal scentedness of the traditional basil leaves. The anchovy fillets provide a counterbalancing salty intensity, though if you're making this for vegetarians, simply leave them out and add a couple of tablespoons of grated pecorino instead (or indeed just bolster the parmesan quantities). Finally, and importantly, the ricotta's milky calmness perfectly offsets the ferocious tangle of ingredients that precedes it, providing just the right amount of mellow creaminess.

I tend to use tagliolini that's been tinted green with spinach here but I have to say this is for reasons more visual than culinary. You neither have to go for the green, nor indeed use tagliolini to start with. Any pasta you like will do. One thing, though: you must make the pesto at the last minute (not hard) and use immediately; the sauce loses its intensity, and thus its point, on standing.

**500g tagliolini verdi**

**50g rocket leaves**

**1 fat or 2 small cloves garlic, peeled**

**30g pine nuts**

**3 anchovy fillets**

**25g parmesan or pecorino, freshly grated**

**100ml extra virgin olive oil**

**1 tablespoon ricotta cheese**

Heat a large pan of salted water and cook the pasta. Put all the other ingredients except for the olive oil and the ricotta into the bowl of the food processor fitted with the double-bladed knife and blitz to a purée. With the motor running, slowly pour the oil down the funnel, till you have a feltily green emulsion. Remove the lid, stir with a spatula to combine the oily puddle which will have collected around the blades and then dollop in the ricotta. Put the lid back on and blitz for a final few seconds, then tip into a bowl and stir to mix well.

You should be doing all this while the pasta's cooking. Once it's ready, drain and dress with this intense, baize-green emulsion.

Serves 6 as a starter; 4 as a main course.

I am a completely shameless solicitor for recipes: I don't restrict myself to bothering just my friends and colleagues, but open the field to include any of their friends and colleagues too (indeed, anyone). This recipe finds its way here by just such a route. It was sent via a friend of my producer, David Edgar, one Geoff Metzker (to whom I am very grateful, as you should be, too) who picked it up during his time working for Sky in Rome. This is how this game works: cooking isn't about the suspicious guarding of closely kept secrets but is a matter of sharing, passing on, the almost gossipy dissemination of habits and practices; recipes that are considered high level security documents are not recipes that survive (or ones, frankly, that you'd want to eat).

The bare ingredients don't look much maybe, but everything comes together, without fuss, in the pan, on the plate: the perfect sauce when every tomato in the shop is tight-shouldered and unluscious.

**6 tablespoons extra virgin olive oil**
**3 cloves garlic, cut into slivers**
**400g tin chopped tomatoes**
**125ml stock (Marigold vegetable**
 **bouillon powder and water is just fine)**

**bunch fresh flat-leaf parsley, roughly**
 **chopped**
**salt and pepper**
**500g rigatoni**

Put a large pan of salted water on to boil for the pasta.

Heat the oil and gently fry the garlic over low to medium heat. When it begins to take on a golden colour – though don't let it scorch – add the tomatoes and turn up the heat. Stir in the stock and let it bubble away, reducing the sauce until it becomes quite lumpy and oily; this should take no more than about 10 minutes. Take the pan off the heat and (just before serving) add the parsley. Taste for seasoning, too, of course.

Meanwhile, cook the rigatoni following the instructions on the packet, and then toss the pasta into the sauce in the pan. Combine everything well and serve straightaway.

Serves 6 for a starter; 4 for a main course.

Left, Pappardelle with Courgettes, Sultanas and Pine Nuts; right, Tagliolini al Pesto Amaro; centre, Spaghettini al Sugo Crudo

In Italy, pasta *al sugo*, pasta with a sauce, means *the* sauce, tomato sauce and this, when the tomatoes are raw, and the sauce is more of a fragrant, olive-oil-soused salad tumbled over hot pasta, is my favourite variant. It's the first thing I make when I hit Italy, not just because this is best eaten under an Italian sun, but because this is best made with Italian tomatoes – by which I mean tomatoes that taste of tomatoes. Actually, it is easier to come by those here than it used to be, but the utmost vigilance is still required: I like tomatoes that are a bit smaller than the palm of my hand, preferably with stalk and indeed stem still attached, and I never, under any circumstances, keep them in the fridge.

| | |
|---|---|
| **1 kg fabulous tomatoes** | **1 clove garlic** |
| **1 teaspoon caster sugar** | **125ml extra virgin olive oil** |
| **Maldon salt** | **500g spaghettini** |
| **black pepper** | |

Blanch the tomatoes by putting them in a large bowl, pouring over boiling water from a kettle to cover, and letting them sit for a few minutes. Drain them, peel them (the blanching makes this easy: just cut with the tip of a knife and the skins will come away easily) then halve them and scoop out the pips. Cut away the cores (this is probably easier once you've quartered them) then chop them; I use my mezzaluna for this, though an ordinary sharp knife would do just fine. Scoop them up, put them in a bowl, stir in the sugar and sprinkle with Maldon salt and grind in some pepper. Lean on the garlic clove with the flat side of a knife to bruise it and peel off the skin and add the smashed clove to the tomatoes in the bowl along with the oil. Stir together brutally with a fork – though I tend to use my Magiwhisk (like a small whisk made of a beard-shaped coil of wire) for this; I want to beat this into more of a sauce – and cover with clingfilm and leave, out of the fridge, for at least half an hour and up to 8 hours.

Cook the pasta according to the packet instructions and once drained, pick out the garlic clove from the tomatoes in the bowl and throw it away, tossing the soused tomatoes into the hot spaghettini. I don't like grated parmesan with this, but I often make it (as per the picture on page 34) with a ball of buffalo mozzarella, diced and stirred into the tomato sauce a minute before combining sauce and pasta. When I'm in Tuscany, I like to use instead a handful of diced pecorino toscano, which is softer, crumblier and sweeter and with a creamier tang than the hard, sharp pecorino Romano used for usual grating (and in the capellini con cacio e pepe on page 40). This is also wonderful, and helps with less fulsomely tomatoey tomatoes, when you add the juice of half a lemon to the tomatoes in the bowl and grate over the zest of a lemon as you toss the pasta in the sauce at the end. Needless to say – I'd presume – any of these variants taste wonderful with a handful of basil leaves, shredded or torn up at the last minute (otherwise they'll start to blacken), some tossed through the sauce before it goes on to the pasta, and some scattered over the pasta afterwards.

Serves 6 as a starter; 4 as a light main course.

## SPAGHETTI AGLIO OLIO PEPERONCINO

I have ummed and erred internally – and sometimes, I'm afraid rumblingly out loud – over whether to include this here or not. On the one hand, pasta with a bit of garlic, olive oil and dried red chilli pepper is hardly a recipe, but on the other, I can't imagine summer without it. I am not someone who wants to eat just cold food when it's hot: I want to sit in the garden with a quickly made bowlful of something heat-infused and fiery. And this is simply the culmination, and almost instant gratification, of that desire.

Besides, since when has ease of execution been a factor militating against any recipe?

**150g spaghetti**
**Maldon salt**
**3–4 tablespoons extra virgin olive oil**
**1 fat clove garlic, or 2 smaller, peeled**
**and sliced thinly lengthwise**

**1 dried red chilli pepper or fat pinch dried**
**red chilli pepper flakes (or to taste)**
**chopped fresh parsley (optional)**

Put a pan of water on the heat to boil for the pasta. When it's come to the boil, add salt and then the spaghetti. When you're about 3 minutes away from the pasta being ready, add the oil and garlic slices to another pan, crumble in the dried chilli pepper and cook over low to medium heat, stirring with a wooden spoon. Once the garlic has taken on a light golden colour, which will hardly take any time, add a couple of tablespoons of pasta-cooking water, stir well with your wooden spoon and turn off the heat. Tip in the cooked, drained spaghetti and toss well so that it's well slicked by the garlic-studded, chilli-flecked sauce. Sprinkle with Maldon salt and some freshly chopped parsley, if you have some to hand, and eat.

Serves 1.

You know, I'd eaten this a couple of times and made it myself (throwing in handfuls of peppery watercress as I did so) a few more before I realised it was, give or take, the River Cafe's recipe – by which I mean to say that although the amounts and full list of ingredients vary, it is an English seaside version of their fabulous original. I suppose that's how you know something's become a classic: it just seeps its way into the culinary language.

Crab is, I think, hugely underrated – so much better than lobster, and much cheaper. You can use frozen crab meat for this, but it's best to get a fishmonger to cook and pick out the meat for you.

Don't let the fact that a pestle and mortar is indicated put you off: this is fabulously easy to make.

2 cloves garlic

1 scant tablespoon Maldon salt

1 large red chilli

1.25kg undressed crab, to give you
    200g white meat and 100g
    brown meat

125ml extra virgin olive oil

juice and zest of 1 lemon

500g linguine

handful fresh parsley, chopped

handful watercress leaves, roughly torn

Put a large pan of water on to boil for the pasta.

In a large pestle and mortar pulverise the peeled garlic cloves with the salt, so that it makes a smooth paste. Then add the chopped and seeded chilli and crush again until you have a gloriously red-tinged mixture. Tip in the crab meat, breaking it up gently with a fork, and pour in the oil. Zest the lemon into the mortar and then add the juice.

Using a fork, beat well to mix, and then you are ready to cook your pasta. So do so, and then drain the pasta and tip into a warmed serving bowl. Immediately pour over the crab sauce and toss the pasta about in it, then throw in the parsley and watercress and toss again.

Serves 6 as a starter; 4 as a main course.

# CAPELLINI CON CACIO E PEPE

This is another gloriously simple, intensely flavoured pasta, best eaten quickly and hungrily under a warm sun though the deep heat of the pepper is gratifyingly warming on cold winter nights. I list pecorino here, rather than parmesan, simply because, in the first instance, that's how I came across it (in Rome, many summers ago) and, in the second, because I love its sharper, sourer edge. Sometimes, though, I use the parmesan I always have hanging about, with the zest of a lemon, or half of one, grated in alongside.

You need the black pepper really quite coarsely ground here (though not quite so coarsely as to induce a coughing fit) so if you can't adjust your pepper mill, bash some peppercorns about in a pestle and mortar instead.

**300g capellini**
**salt**
**15g unsalted butter**

**10 tablespoons (about 50g) freshly
  grated pecorino Romano**
**1 tablespoon black peppercorns,
  coarsely ground**

Put a panful of water on to boil for the pasta; once it's come to the boil, add salt then the pasta and cook according to the instructions on the packet. Just before you drain it, though, remove a coffee cupful of its cooking water.

So, drain the pasta and add the butter to the hot pan and then tip in the capellini and toss well, dribbling in a tablespoonful or so of cooking liquid as you do so. Now add the grated pecorino and coarse black pepper and toss well in the residual heat of the pan – adding a little more pasta-cooking liquid if you need the lubrication – before tipping into warmed bowls.

Serves 4 as a starter; or 2 as a main course.

# SHORT PASTA WITH ASPARAGUS, LEMON, GARLIC AND PARSLEY

If there's anything you're going to end up eating, sitting in the garden, throughout summer, it is this. True, new season's asparagus, our own home-grown asparagus, is what you'd use ideally (and this is, incidentally, a very good way of making a relatively small amount of expensive asparagus go far without tasting of economy), but I don't think it's necessary to restrict preparation of this to the short time it's in season. You wouldn't want to eat this in winter when all you can get is thick and fibrous spears from far-flung places, but bits straggling in from here and there later on in summer is nothing to get preciously sniffy about.

The simplicity of this is not just about ease of preparation, gratifying though this is, but about the uncluttered, perfectly balanced arrangement of tastes and texture.

**500g asparagus**
**salt**
**125ml extra virgin olive oil**
**2 cloves garlic, finely chopped**
**juice and zest of half a large lemon**

**500g rigatoni or penne or any short, stubby pasta you want**
**2 tablespoons chopped fresh flat-leaf parsley**

Snap the woody stems off the bottom of the asparagus, and cut the remaining stalk lengthways and diagonally at 2cm intervals, leaving the tip whole. If it is possible, find a large saucepan to cook the pasta in, that can fit a steamer on top. Bring the saucepan to the boil, add salt generously, and steam the asparagus for 2 minutes. Obviously, you can use two separate pans if you want, but there's something pleasing about dovetailing the operation. And I know that steaming the asparagus means it will be no longer hot when you toss it in the pasta, but I don't mind that; if you do, put it in the microwave for a few seconds – go slowly just till it's warm, otherwise you run the risk of overcooking it – to reheat when you drain the pasta later.

Put the oil in a frying pan and gently turn the garlic golden over a pretty low heat – you neither want the garlic to burn and turn acrid nor the oil to lose its robustness of flavour – then add the lemon juice, stir and take off the heat. Meanwhile cook the rigatoni, or whatever, in the big pan of water, and when it is al dente, drain and pour into the frying pan. Add the asparagus, toss everything about, sprinkling with the parsley and not-too-finely grated lemon zest.

If you're serving the pasta in a bowl (rather than just serving it straight from the pan – and there's nothing wrong in that) remember to heat it first, and add the parsley and lemon zest only after the pasta's been transferred.

Serves 6 as a starter; 4 as a main course.

You might label this shiny black muss+led variation of linguine alle vongole, linguine alle cozze, but to be frank, this version is not very Italian-flavoured. It owes something to the French taste for moules marinière, and reaches Spainwards for a slug of sherry, in place of the usual white wine, to add oomph to the molluscs' briney juices.

It helps if you can get small mussels, simply because otherwise you get too much clattery shell per strand of pasta, but it's not a life-or-death stipulation. Mussels that are sold in already cleaned and debarnacled bags tend to be reasonably sized. You do have to soak them in cold water in the sink (mussels that stay open at this stage need to be jettisoned, just as mussels that fail to open once they're on the heat have to be chucked later), and you might have to scrape off a few bits of beard and barnacle that cling to the shells, but it's unlikely, these days, to be much of a job.

| | |
|---|---|
| 500g small mussels | 1 fresh long red chilli, deseeded and cut |
| salt | into strips |
| 250g linguine | 100ml Amontillado sherry |
| 2–3 tablespoons olive oil | 2–3 tablespoons chopped fresh parsley |
| 1 clove garlic, cut into shards | |

Put the mussels to soak in a sinkful of cold water – using a knife to scrape off any bits of beard or barnacle that cling to the shells – while you heat the water for the pasta. When the water comes to the boil, add salt and then, when boiling again, the linguine. Cook them until nearly ready: you're going to give them a minute or so later to continue cooking with the mussels and their briney, winey juices.

So, while the pasta's cooking, drain the mussels, discarding those that remain open when you rap the shells, and sit them in a colander for a while. Get out a large pan (big enough to fit all the pasta in later) and pour in the oil. Add the garlic shards and strips of chilli pepper and heat over a lowish flame till warmly sizzling, but don't let the garlic brown or it will become bitter and acrid. Tip the mussels clatteringly into the garlic and chilli pan, turn up the heat, pour in the sherry and clamp shut with a lid. Shake the pan a couple of times, just to disperse the heat, but not so much that you fracture the shells. In a few minutes, the mussels should be steamed open; any that stay resolutely shut are bad and you must just pick through them and throw them away.

Add the drained, almost-cooked pasta, put the lid on again and swirl about. In another minute or so, the pasta will have cooked to the requisite tough tenderness – the joy of linguine is that it keeps a certain robust and satisfying chewy mouth-fillingness – and will have absorbed much of the garlicky, smokey-sherried mussel juices, and be swellingly bound in a wonderful Riviera-redolent sea syrup. But if the pasta looks like it needs a little more time, just shove the lid on again and give it another minute or so. The thing here is to let everything, quite simply, come together.

Add half the parsley, shake the pan to distribute evenly, and turn into a large bowl, sprinkling, finally, with the rest of the parsley. You do not offer cheese with this pasta; I am not generally good with authority, but some rules – such as the Italian one that forbids the addition of cheese to any pasta sauce containing fish – hold good.

Serves 2 or, sometimes, just this one.

## LINGUINE ALLE VONGOLE

To cook yourself a glorious bowlful of this, you just follow the recipe above, substituting a crumbled dried red chilli – I just prefer it with this – for the fresh one above and in place of the mussels, use 300g palourde clams (their shells weigh less, so you don't need as much in weight) and instead of the sherry use white wine or vermouth diluted with a little water.

## GREEKISH LAMB PASTA

This is not-quite spag bol but a warming but still summery one-course supper for evenings when the sun is shining, but not so fiercely as to make slow-cooked meatiness an unseasonable abomination. In truth, I wouldn't like to claim that this oregano-flecked, feta-topped meat sauce *is* really Greek, but a Greek friend of mine (admittedly deracinated, and educated in England) used to make something like it. If it makes life easier, you can cook the lamb mince in advance, seeing to the pasta and reheating the sauce and crumbling over the astringent white cheese at the last minute. And it is a wonderful combination: the salty-sourness of the feta and sweetness of the tomatoey, oregano-redolent lamb meld fabulously, persuasively together. I don't usually go in for meat sauces with pasta hugely, but this is heavenly, food for the (Greek) Gods.

1 large onion
4 cloves garlic
150g button mushrooms
2 tablespoons dried oregano
2 tablespoons olive oil
500g lamb mince
250ml red wine
2 x 400g tins tomatoes

1 tablespoon tomato purée mixed with 2 tablespoons milk
1 tablespoon caster sugar
salt and black pepper
500g spaghetti, spaghettini, linguine or tagliatelle
200g feta cheese

Blitz the onion, garlic, mushrooms and a tablespoon of the dried oregano to rubble in the processor, or just chop finely by hand. Cook in the oil in a frying pan which will take the meat later for about 10 minutes on a low-to-medium heat, until softened. Don't panic if it looks as if you've got a ridiculously vast panful at first: it will cook down to a more modest amount. Push the cooked onion and mushroom mixture to the sides when softened, and add the minced lamb to the pan, stirring and prodding with your wooden spoon until the raw colour has lost its edge. Add the wine and let it bubble up for a minute or so. Then add the tomatoes, the tomato purée which you've diluted with the milk, the remaining tablespoon of oregano, the sugar, a teaspoon or so of salt and a good grinding of pepper. Stir well, so that the tomatoes break up and everything is mixed together, cover and cook for at least 30 minutes over a lowish heat. That's to say, all meat sauces like this are better the longer they're (slowly) cooked, but don't worry if you've got only half an hour.

Meanwhile, put a copious amount of water to boil in the largest pan you've got. When it's boiling, salt well and cook the pasta according to taste and packet instructions. While it's cooking, chop or crumble the feta (I use my mezzaluna here) and warm a large bowl or plate (just filling it with hot water in the sink's fine). When the pasta's ready, drain it and toss it with a ladleful or so of the meat sauce. Turn into the warmed (and dried) bowl or plate, push towards the edges and pour the rest of the meat sauce on top and in the middle. Crumble over the chopped feta and serve, immediately.

Serves 6 as a starter; 4 as a main course.

# BAKED PASTA SHELLS STUFFED WITH SPINACH AND RICOTTA

I admit that stuffed pasta, swathed in tomato sauce and baked in the oven doesn't *look* summery, but the point is this: the tomato sauce that dresses the pasta is light and fresh; the ricotta and spinach within it are lighter and fresher still. It's fiddly to make, I'll grant you, but there is a calming, ritualistic aspect to it that makes it strangely unflustering to put together in anything but the most scorching summer heat. Besides, I like this best left to sit for a while once it's done its time in the oven, so that you eat it warm rather than hot; strangely enough – given the amount of green stuff in it – so do my children.

You can make this in advance – that's to say, cook and stuff the pasta and sit it in its sauce and leave it, covered in the fridge for a few hours, before adding the final bit of parmesan and baking it in the oven – which can make life easier if you've got a huge tableful of people coming over later. To be honest, this is the sort of pasta you give people as a main course, with nothing but an astringently dressed crisp green salad.

1 clove garlic, minced

1 onion, finely chopped

3 tablespoons olive oil

2 x 700g bottles tomato passata

700g fresh spinach (or 1kg frozen chopped spinach, thawed and thoroughly drained)

500g ricotta

2 eggs, beaten

1 x 100g piece parmesan

freshly grated nutmeg

salt and pepper

500g large pasta shells

Preheat the oven to 200°C/gas mark 6.

In a very large saucepan, gently fry the garlic and onion in the oil for about 5–10 minutes until translucent. Add the passata and refill both bottles with water about three-quarters full, giving them a good shake to mop up any tomato. This will give you about 1.2 litres water. Add it to the pan. Bring the sauce to the boil and then partially cover and simmer for about 25 minutes.

Soak the fresh spinach in some cold water in the sink to get rid of any mud, drain and then cook in just the water that's still clinging to the leaves until it has wilted down and cooked through, then drain well and chop roughly (you can just go at it with scissors while it's sitting in the colander). If you're using frozen chopped spinach, make sure – once it's thawed – that you've pressed out every last bit of water; you can also use frozen leaf spinach, and chop it yourself once it's thawed and drained.

Empty the ricotta into a bowl, add the eggs and then grate in about 75g of the parmesan. Add the spinach when it is cool, squeezing out (again) any excess water with your hands, then stir everything together and season it well with the nutmeg and salt and pepper.

Cook the pasta shells in a large pan of water, for about 5 minutes once they have come back to the boil, then drain and leave them to get cool enough for you to stuff them without burning your fingers. Tip the shells into a dish, of approximately 38 x 32cm, so that they lie in a single layer, then fill each shell with a heaped teaspoon of the spinach and ricotta filling. Ladle the tomato sauce over the pasta, and grate over the remaining parmesan.

Bake for about 20–30 minutes by which time the pasta will be tender and the light tomato sauce hot and bubbling. Remove from the oven and let stand for a while to cool down slightly before serving.

Serves 8–10.

I love the Japanese way of eating cold noodles: I just lift a bowl to my face, fork furiously and slurp. If you want to make these part of a meal, then know that they go wonderfully well with salmon: just get some fillets, sear them in a hot pan, leaving the interior fleshily coral. But I love eating these as they are, in huge quantities and – preferably – alone. Because they're served cold, you can profitably keep leftovers for midnight fridge-raiding later. Boxed into foil containers, they are the perfect, if unconventional, food to take along for a picnic.

**75g sesame seeds**
**salt**
**250g soba noodles**
**2 teaspoons rice vinegar**

**5 teaspoons soy sauce**
**2 teaspoons honey**
**2 teaspoons sesame oil**
**5 spring onions**

Toast the sesame seeds in a dry pan over a high heat until they look golden brown, and tip them into a bowl.

Bring a large pan of water to the boil and add some salt. Put in the soba noodles and cook them for about 6 minutes (or according to packet instructions) until they are tender but not mushy. Have a bowl of iced water waiting to plunge them into after draining.

In the bowl you are going to serve them in, mix the vinegar, soy sauce, honey and oil. Then finely slice the spring onions and put them into the bowl with the cooled, drained noodles and mix together thoroughly before adding the sesame seeds and tossing again.

Leave the sesame seed noodles for about half an hour to let the flavours develop, although this is not absolutely necessary or sometimes even possible.

Serves 4 as part of a meal; or 2 when eaten, gratifyingly, as they are.

SALADS

# OLD-FASHIONED TOMATO SALAD

This tomato salad is all you need for a summer starter. What I do is take the tomatoes out into the garden, uncut, on a flat plate or two, for an hour before I want to make the salad: it takes any chill off them and makes them taste somehow more tomatoey. Cherry tomatoes perhaps sound new-fangled rather than old-fashioned, but I'm coming to that. For the dressing is, and I refuse to apologise for it, nothing more nor less than that great – though, now that we live in the extra-virgin age, greatly discredited – item from the English culinary canon, Salad Cream. Banish all childhood memories of sick-flavoured gloop in a jar: this is worlds and E-additives apart. The recipe I give for it is by and large adapted from Margaret Costa: I have substituted tarragon vinegar, which I prefer here, but do use cider vinegar, as she stipulates, if you want. Any leftover salad cream can be stored in the fridge in an old jam jar; indeed you may find you want to make double the amount below, so well will it go down.

It's hardly English, but I use Italian 00 flour (available at supermarkets now) instead of plain flour because it loses its flouriness with less cooking than does our coarser-milled home-grown variety, but it's not worth losing sleep over.

**500g good cherry tomatoes, halved**

**quarter teaspoon made English mustard or pinch mustard powder**

**1 heaped tablespoon 00 or plain flour**

**1 teaspoon caster sugar**

**salt and black pepper**

**250ml full-fat milk**

**1 egg, beaten**

**4 tablespoons tarragon vinegar**

**1 tablespoon sunflower oil**

**chives or green parts of spring onions**

Half fill a sink with cold water.

Combine the mustard, flour and sugar, with about a teaspoon of salt and a good grinding of pepper, in a heavy-based saucepan. Add a little of the milk and stir to mix to a smooth paste, then put on a gentle heat and keep adding the milk, and stirring as you do so. I find my Magiwhisk the best thing to banish lumpiness here, but it's not a difficult operation whatever you use.

When all the milk's in, add the beaten egg and vinegar and keep on whisking until it's beginning to thicken. When the mixture's got the texture of single cream, whisk in the oil then plunge the pan in the sink of cold water and continue whisking for a while. When it's cool (you can pour into a bowl then put the bowl over ice if you want speedy cooling), cut the tomatoes in half and arrange on one huge plate or two fairly large ones. Drizzle a few spoonfuls over (don't drench: think Jackson Pollock) then add some chopped spring onions or chives. Unexpected heaven.

Serves 6.

I am convinced that it is when raw that beetroot is at its best, and this recipe offers the most persuasive evidence; I promise you that it is loved even by those who were traumatised by putridly sweet and vinegary school beetroot. The dill and mustard seed here resonate with Scandinavian flavours, and for this reason I most often serve it alongside the seared mustard-coated salmon and Hasselback potatoes (see pages 97 and 151). But if you can't find fresh dill or just shudderingly abominate it, use flat-leaf parsley in its place. At any rate, the salad lends itself to whatever herby combination you're in the mood for; I just as often go the Stephanie Alexander route (in whose *Cook's Companion* I discovered the sweet nuttiness and tang of uncooked, grated beet) by forgoing the mustard seeds and dill and bunging in instead, fresh leafy mounds of chopped coriander and mint.

**big bunch fresh dill (to yield about 6 tablespoons when chopped)**
**500g raw beetroot**
**juice of 1 lemon**

**2 tablespoons extra virgin olive oil**
**2 tablespoons mustard seeds**
**a spoonful or so of chopped fresh flat-leaf parsley (optional)**

I always make this in the food processor, not because it's necessary, but just because it makes life easier. Put quite a wodge of dill, without stalks, in the processor with the double-bladed knife fitted and blitz till finely chopped. About 6 tablespoons seems to me the right amount for this quantity of beetroot, but a bit here or there makes no difference. Scrape it out into a large bowl (keeping a small amount on one side for sprinkling later) and then fit, if you have one, the julienne disc, or if not, the grater disc. Peel the beetroot and chop it into chunks that will fit down the funnel; I use rubber gloves for this, so I'm not like Lady Macbeth with my incarnadined hands forever.

When all the beetroot is grated, turn it into the bowl with the dill and toss so both are mixed well together. Squeeze the lemon juice over, drizzle in the olive oil and toss again. When everything is well but lightly combined, put a non-stick or heavy-based frying pan on the heat and toast the mustard seeds for a couple of minutes. Add to the beetroot and dill salad and, again, toss well. Turn out to a bowl or plate – I always prefer salads on a plate – and scatter your little bit of reserved dill over, adding a little chopped fresh parsley, if you have some to hand, for a final uplifting hit of more vibrant green.

Serves 6.

# BAKED POTATO SALAD

If the idea of a baked potato salad sounds ludicrous, let me attempt to reassure you. It is not in fact cooked, but rather evolved. It came about because I had a couple of leftover baked potatoes in the fridge one day, and although there are few things I like more than cold potatoes, sprinkled with Maldon salt and freshly ground black pepper, then smeared, bite by bite, while still standing at the fridge, with unsalted butter, I decided to make something a little more ceremonious, but scarcely more labour-intensive, out of them. It's so good that I'd think nothing now of baking potatoes, then leaving them around to cool, especially for it.

Sumac, should you not have come across it before, is a dark red berry, ground to make a powder of aromatic, citrussy intensity. Use it once and you'll find an excuse to add it more and more in your cooking: somehow it provides sharpness and mellow depth at the same time.

| | |
|---|---|
| **2 baked potatoes** | **half teaspoon cumin** |
| **4 tablespoons extra virgin olive oil** | **1 spring onion, sliced** |
| **juice of half a lemon** | **lots of Maldon salt** |
| **half teaspoon sumac** | **chopped fresh parsley (optional)** |

Cut the baked potatoes in half and roughly scoop out the flesh on to a plate with a spoon. Don't worry about bringing some of the scorched skin along with you; it aids appearance and taste and besides, this is a rough and ramshackle kind of a dish.

Spoon over the olive oil and squeeze over the lemon, then sprinkle over the sumac, cumin and sliced spring onion. Salt generously, and by all means add some freshly chopped parsley (or indeed coriander) if you want.

Serves about 3, depending on what's being eaten alongside.

# CACIK

Pronounced 'jajek', this is simply Turkish tsatsiki: cucumber salad, hot with garlic, but made coolly soothing with yoghurt and mint. I love it best with lamb, sweet pink loins of it, seared on the grill and then cut into tender rags, or dolloped alongside thick slices cut off a whole, roast, deeply-spiced leg, but this is not intended to be a limiting recommendation.

One constraint exists, however: don't leave this hanging around too long. It's true that the cucumber will get watery and make the salad too liquid after a while, but the real problem is that the raw garlic, once no-longer freshly minced, runs the risk of turning acrid. I'm not saying I don't *like* eating it, spooned straight from leftover, fridge-bound bowl to mouth late at night, I just feel like I ought to be wearing a surgical mask afterwards.

| | |
|---|---|
| 1 cucumber | leaves from 1 bunch fresh mint, chopped |
| 500g Greek yoghurt | 1–2 cloves garlic, depending on size |
| 1 teaspoon dried mint | and intensity |
| 1–2 teaspoons salt | extra virgin olive oil to drizzle over |

Peel and dice the cucumber finely and add to the yoghurt in a mixing bowl. Stir in the dried mint, salt and most of the fresh mint, microplane in the garlic (or finely mince it), stir again, then tip the whole thing into a serving dish. Sprinkle over the last scrapings of chopped mint and drizzle with the oil.

It's difficult to say how many this serves, as it all depends on how you like to eat it. I love it – to add to the introductory guidance above – as a mayonnaise substitute in sandwiches, as a dip for tortilla chips, spooned plateside as a sauce-like salad. But if this is part of a mezze, then this amount should do just fine for a desirably greedy group of about 8 at least.

This is not the place for in-depth social history, unless you take the view – as I do – that all food is social history, but I do need to provide a bit of provenance. Once upon a time there was Biba, an ill-lit but fabulous boutique, shoplifters' paradise, at the top of Kensington High Street. It moved, triumphantly, down the road to the old Derry and Tom's building, four or five huge floors of it, and on the fourth, or fifth, I can't remember, was its restaurant, the Rainbow Room, where my mother took me for treats when I was a child, while she kitted herself out in suede boots, maxi-coats and mini-dresses. This salad, or some approximation of it, was on its menu and my mother loved it and made her own version at home regularly. I do, too. Its ingredients list may sound odd, but this is a combination that not only works but becomes addictive. Don't be alarmed at the amount of vinegar: the astringency of the dressing, against the fulsome oiliness of the nuts and, in turn, nutty sweetness of the carrots, is the whole point.

**4 medium carrots, peeled**

**75g salted peanuts**

**2 tablespoons red wine vinegar**

**2 tablespoons groundnut oil**

**few drops sesame oil**

Grate the carrots very coarsely, push them through the french-fry cutter in the processor, or just cut them into skinny batons. In a bowl, combine them with the peanuts and then add the remaining ingredients. I like to eat this, straight out of the Pyrex pudding basin I mix it in, held up high, under my chin, for ease of eating-action. In fact, the only way I stop eating it is by having someone prise the bowl out of my hands.

Serves 1–2, depending on your compulsiveness or generosity.

# DOUBLE COURGETTE AND BEAN SALAD

The double component is that both courgette and bean elements are twofold: yellow and green courgettes, cut into batons, oil-dressed and oven-roasted; waxy, kidney-curling vibrantly green broad beans, and darker green fine beans, both lightly boiled then refreshed to keep their verdant intensity. It's a salad just in the sense that all the vegetables are left to get to room temperature – though certainly no colder – before being spritzed with lemon and tossed with basil and parsley: early summer on a plate.

**1kg yellow courgettes**
**500g green courgettes**
**approx. 80ml olive oil**
**750g fresh broad beans, podded and –**
**I'm sorry – shelled (or 250g frozen**
**broad beans, shelled)**

**250g fine green beans**
**salt and pepper**
**juice of 1 lemon**
**bunch fresh basil**
**bunch fresh parsley**

Preheat the oven to 200°C/gas mark 6.

Cut all the courgettes into 3 then cut each third into batons. Arrange them in a large roasting tin and coat them well with the oil. Frankly, the best way to do this is to pour the oil over and then smoosh everything about in the tin with your hands. Stick the tin in the oven and roast the courgettes for about 30 minutes, by which time they should be cooked through and golden at the edges.

While this is going on, cook the broad beans (and it truly is worth popping them out of their skins; see directions for the minestrone on page 26) and fine beans separately in salted boiling water until tender, then drain and refresh them both by plunging them in iced water and then draining them again.

When the courgettes are cool, put them in a bowl with the two beans and dress them with lemon juice; the courgettes should be sufficiently, and desirably, oily to need no extra drizzling here. Chop the basil and parsley and add them to the bowl, mixing everything gently (again, just hands is easiest) to avoid squashing the courgette batons.

Check the seasoning and add salt and pepper as needed, decant into a clean serving dish and sprinkle over whatever bits of basil and parsley are clinging to the chopping board.

Serves 4–6.

Greek salad is the sort of abominated fixture in the culinary canon which no appetite for retro-chic can make cool. Forget about all that, because a good Greek salad is, not surprisingly, made for languorous picking at in the heat. Whenever I make this, it's met, at first, with just slightly patronising amusement – and then the most colossal greed. I think the trick is twofold: substitute sliced fennel for the more traditional cucumber (which also has the benefit of not making the salad go wet and soggy on standing around); and let the onion steep, sprinkled with dried oregano, in the oil and vinegar for long enough for it to lose any potential for that acrid, rib-sticking aftertaste. This version is mild, abundant, gloriously summery. If you don't like fennel, then just leave it out, but exclude, still, the cucumber.

| | |
|---|---|
| **1 red onion** | **pinch of Maldon salt** |
| **1 tablespoon dried oregano** | **1 very large cos lettuce** |
| **black pepper** | **1 bulb fennel** |
| **1 tablespoon red wine vinegar** | **125g pitted black olives** |
| **200ml extra virgin olive oil** | **400g feta cheese** |
| **5 good tomatoes** | **juice of half a lemon** |
| **1 teaspoon caster sugar** | |

Peel and finely slice the red onion then sprinkle over the oregano and grind over some pepper. Pour in the vinegar and oil and toss well, cover with clingfilm and leave to steep for a good 2 hours; longer's fine. What you'll notice, once it's had its time, as well, is that the blooded crimson of the onion is somehow now a luminescent puce. It's a science thing, something to do with the acid in the vinegar: don't ask. You don't need to be fully conversant with the technicalities to be able to take advantage of them. That's to say, I often use this trick in other ways. An otherwise overwhelmingly brown slab of meat can be immediately lifted (in looks and taste) by being covered with some red onions, cut into wedges of 8 or so, and then fried in olive oil, to which, once softened, you add the juice of a lemon. On top of the lemony pink onions add some sprinkled Maldon salt and a generous amount of summer-green chopped parsley. Or make a quick sauce for pasta (this should be enough for a 500g packet of spaghetti) by cutting a red onion into very fine half-moons (ie, cut the onion in half and then slice each half as finely as you can), frying it in olive oil, spritzing in the juice of half a lemon, as before, and then tossing this, along with 200g tuna cut into thin little rags, into the cooked drained spaghetti; the heat of the pasta will cook the raw tuna plenty. Add seasoning to taste, and some extra virgin olive oil as you like, and a goodish amount of chopped fresh parsley (again). But these are just suggestions: the pink onion technique can be drawn on in whatever way pleases you.

But to return to the case in hand: when you want to eat, get started with the rest of the salad. Cut the tomatoes into quarters, then cut each quarter into quarters (always lengthwise) again, so that you have a collection of very fine segments (rather than chunks). Sprinkle the sugar and a pinch of salt over them and leave while you get on with the rest. Wash the lettuce if you need to (I always try and get away with not) tear into big pieces and put into a large, wide salad bowl. Slice the fennel and add that, then the olives and the feta, cut or crumbled into rough chunks, and toss well. Now add the tomatoes, the red onion – now lucidly pink – in its marinade-dressing and the lemon juice. Toss gently, but thoroughly, so that everything is well combined.

This is addictive: you will find yourself making it all through summer – and beyond.

Serves 6–8.

There is something about the resonant graininess of pulses that, when eaten at balmy room temperature, makes me think immediately of a lingering, wide-skied, late-summer supper. You can pretty well fiddle about with this as you wish: if you want to use feta in place of chèvre, fine by me; equally, coriander works well instead of mint (both dried and fresh); forget the sweet, soft peppers if you want; add some chopped fresh tomatoes if the idea appeals. I'm easy. So should you be. But there is one unignorable stipulation: you must use proper, authentic Puy lentils, not any other type or even healthstore-packaged ones thus erroneously, and misleadingly, named. The real things are from France and the box bears the stamp of authentication: it's not that other varieties are lesser, they just get fuzzy around the edges on cooking and this salad loses a little of its appeal when an element of sludge is introduced.

**275g goat's cheese (about 6cm cut from a goat's cheese log, approx. 8cm in diameter)**
**1 lemon**
**8 tablespoons extra virgin olive oil**
**1 teaspoon dried mint**
**500g Puy lentils**

**1 onion**
**3–4 cloves garlic**
**1 tablespoon chilli oil**
**Maldon salt**
**1 x 325g jar sweet peppers in oil**
**bunch fresh mint, chopped**

Crumble the goat's cheese and marinate in the juice and zest of half the lemon, half the olive oil and the dried mint.

Put the lentils in a large saucepan of water and add the onion, halved, along with the garlic cloves and chilli oil. Cook for about 25 minutes or until tender – be certain to check after about 18 minutes and then drain.

Pour the remaining olive oil over the warm lentils, season with salt, and add the juice and zest of the remaining half lemon. Drain the peppers and mix them into the lentils, which I find easiest to do with my hands; for one thing, it makes you less likely to crush the lentils.

When the salad has reached room temperature, add the marinated goat's cheese and sprinkle over the fresh chopped mint.

Serves 6–8.

# ITALIAN BEETROOT SALAD

I came across this in the great late Jane Grigson's *Vegetable Book*, and it serves as a reminder that we, like children, need to be shaken out of our squeamish food prejudices. There's something about the flabby, sweet, cooked flesh of beetroot that's always slightly spooked me but the robust simplicity of this – the plain, but striking arrangement of just beetroot, onion, mint, olive oil and red wine vinegar – has made me override, completely, my raw-beetroot-salad-only rule.

You do have to be picky about the beetroot, though. Buy it cooked by all means, but make sure it's not lethally macerated in brine or vinegar; vacuum-packed is fine, and these tend to be smaller and nuttier in taste than those monstrous globes I remember from school.

As in the Greek Salad on page 62, I like to steep the red onion rings in the vinegar for a while first. To be frank, a quarter of an hour is probably enough to stave off acridness and bring all that glimmering pinkness to the fore which, against the garnet darkness of the beets, produces a satisfaction of its own.

We might not initially consider mint to be a characteristically Italian ingredient, but that is largely because of the culinary domination of the cooking of Northern Italy in recent years: in the South, mint grows in the wild and finds its way, as a matter of course, into the kitchen.

I love this salad particularly with cold duck; a little grated orange zest, sprinkled along with the mint, wouldn't go amiss in this partnership either.

**1 red onion**

**2 x 15ml tablespoons red wine vinegar**

**8 large or 16 small cooked beetroot (about 750g)**

**2 tablespoons extra virgin olive oil**

**3 tablespoons of chopped fresh mint**

**Maldon salt**

Peel the onion and cut it into fine rings, then sit these rings in a shallow bowl and spoon over the red wine vinegar. Cover with clingfilm and leave to steep for at least a quarter of an hour or for up to three.

Slice the beetroot and arrange these rounds on a large plate, top gracefully with the onion rings, pouring over any vinegar from the bowl and then drizzle over the oil and sprinkle with the mint and Maldon salt.

Serves 4–6.

# WATERMELON, FETA AND BLACK OLIVE SALAD

As improbable as it might sound, this combination is utterly fantastic, both savoury and refreshing at the same time. You can pare it down to the essential contrast, and serve no more than a plate of chunked watermelon, sprinkled with feta and mint and spritzed with lime, but this full-length version is hardly troublesome to make and once made will, I assure you, become a regular feature of your summer table.

**1 small red onion**
**2–4 limes, depending on juiciness**
**1.5 kg sweet, ripe watermelon**
**250g feta cheese**
**bunch fresh flat-leaf parsley**

**bunch fresh mint, chopped**
**3–4 tablespoons extra virgin olive oil**
**100g pitted black olives**
**black pepper**

Peel and halve the red onion and cut into very fine half-moons and put in a small bowl to steep with the lime juice, to bring out the transparent pinkness in the onions and diminish their rasp. Two limes' worth should do it, but you can find the fruits disappointingly dried up and barren when you cut them in half, in which case add more.

Remove the rind and pips from the watermelon, and cut into approximately 4cm triangular chunks, if that makes sense (maths is not my strong point). Cut the feta into similar sized pieces and put them both into a large, wide shallow bowl. Tear off sprigs of parsley so that it is used like a salad leaf, rather than a garnish, and add to the bowl along with the chopped mint.

Tip the now glowingly puce onions, along with their pink juices over the salad in the bowl, add the oil and olives, then using your hands toss the salad very gently so that the feta and melon don't lose their shape. Add a good grinding of black pepper and taste to see whether the dressing needs more lime. Hava Negila! The taste of Tel Aviv sunshine!

Serves 8.

# FETA, WALNUT AND HERB SALAD

I call this a salad, with the excuse that these sorts of grainy pastes are often thus described in Greece and the rest of the Eastern Mediterranean from where, give or take, this emanates, but the real reason is that in the struggle between 'dip' and 'purée', neither won out. I urgently needed to convey to you the simple freshness, the raw-depthed flavour, of this combination: once you make it (I won't begin to call it cooking) you'll be convinced, but I didn't want any unseemly word to get in the way before you even start. You might now gather that, however it's named, it's best eaten by sludging it over chunks of raw vegetable, or just by dipping them into it.

**25g each of: fresh mint, parsley and basil**
**200g feta cheese**
**200g shelled walnuts, chopped**
**6 spring onions**

**1 clove garlic**
**half teaspoon salt**
**pepper**
**1 tablespoon lime juice**
**60ml olive oil**

Process all of the above to make a grainy paste. That's it. What are you waiting for?
Serves 4–6 with cruditées.

# SECOND COURSE

## PRAWN AND BLACK RICE SALAD WITH VIETNAMESE DRESSING

This didn't start life quite like this. That's to say, I happened to have a bit of cold black rice and some Vietnamese dipping sauce left over in the fridge one day, along with a fresh consignment of raw, peeled prawns. The black rice had gone with a fish curry; the dipping sauce I'd eaten with a lemongrass-stuffed roast chicken. I'm telling you this simply to illustrate that this is what real cooking is about: you just go with what you've got.

In fact you could play with this a number of ways. You could have the rice hot, the hot prawns, too, just stirred through with the cold dipping sauce-turned-dressing; in place of the prawns, you could have hot, quickly fried squid rings; you could forgo the fish part and turn this vegetarian by adding some soft, jade chunks of avocado to the cold black rice and chilli-speckled dressing. The dipping sauce anyway is something I wouldn't want to live without: I love it with roast or poached chicken, grilled chicken wings, to dunk prawns into, or to spoon over plain steamed pak choi or broccoli. I could go on – and often do.

The black rice is real black rice, not wild rice and not white rice dyed black with squid ink. It's packaged by Merchant Gourmet and I get it from the supermarket, usually without any trouble.

**for the Vietnamese dipping sauce/ dressing:**

2 cloves garlic, minced or crushed

2 fresh Thai birdeye chillies or other red chillies, finely sliced

approx. 4cm fresh ginger, finely minced

4 tablespoons fish sauce

2 tablespoons lime juice (about 1 lime)

4 tablespoons water

2 tablespoons caster sugar

**for the salad:**

250g Nanking black rice

500g raw, peeled prawns

salt

juice of half a lemon

To make the sauce, simply mix all the ingredients together. It doesn't get much less complicated than that, frankly.

Well, there is the small matter of the rice and prawns. The rice you just cook by following the instructions on the packet; the prawns you poach in some simmering salted water, to which you've added the juice of half a lemon, for 5 minutes or so or until just cooked through but still very tender. Let both rice and prawns cool, then give the sauce a quick stir and spoon some over the rice, fork this through and then tumble the prawns on top, spooning a little more sauce over as you go.

Serves 2 as a main course; 4 as a starter.

Mostly I cook in lieu of travelling, but this is my way of reminding myself that I once was that person who sat in the shade on gold sand under blue skies gazing at an ocean bluer still...

This is a sprightly curry, fierily orange and warm with cinnamon and nutmeg. Make some plain basmati rice to go with it and you're done.

**1 tablespoon turmeric**

**1 teaspoon ground coriander**

**1 teaspoon ground cumin**

**half teaspoon chilli powder**

**quarter teaspoon mace**

**4cm piece fresh ginger**

**2 cloves garlic**

**1 onion**

**salt**

**2 tablespoons groundnut oil**

**1 x 400g tin chopped tomatoes**

**juice and zest of half a lemon**

**1 stick cinnamon**

**1 tablespoon curry leaves**

**750g medium raw prawns, shelled and deveined**

**good grating nutmeg**

**handful chopped fresh coriander**

**3–4 green finger chillies**

Measure out the turmeric, coriander, cumin, chilli powder and mace into a bowl and grate over the peeled ginger and garlic cloves with a microplane. Add a little water to form a paste, and then leave to one side. Finely chop the onion, adding a bit of Maldon salt to stop it catching, and fry gently in the oil until it softens. Stir in the spice paste and, stirring still, cook for a minute or so. Pour in the tomatoes, then fill the empty can with water and add it to the pan. Squeeze in the lemon juice and pop in the cinnamon stick and curry leaves, and let the whole sauce simmer gently for about half an hour so that it can thicken and the ground spices will lose their floury taste.

When you are ready to eat – and you can cook the sauce well in advance if this suits – add the raw prawns and let them cook through. Keep tasting them to make sure they have lost their glassy middle.

Pour the curry into a shallow bowl and grate well with fresh nutmeg and the lemon zest. Sprinkle over the coriander, and split the finger chillies lengthwise leaving their stalks and seeds intact (unless you are a wuss about such matters, in which case deseed by all means). Arrange them as artistically as you please over the dish.

Serves 4–6.

You don't need to barbecue the sea bass for this: wrap it in foil and bake it in the oven if that's easier. Similarly, you don't need to use sea bass, which, though delicious, is expensive. The point is, any fish goes with these lemons which are preserved not quite in the usual way of being steeped in salt for weeks but are quickly blanched and then cooked in a light, briney syrup. The advantages are twofold: you can prepare the lemons just the day before you need to use them rather than having to get yourself efficiently ahead of yourself by starting the lemons ten days before (who knows what they're going to do, let alone going to cook, ten days in advance?); and this method tamps down rather than points up their rasping acidity, providing a mellow fruitfulness rather than acerbic tang.

**for the preserved lemons:**

| | |
|---|---|
| 4 unwaxed lemons | 100g Maldon salt |
| 250g caster sugar | 500ml water |

Cut each lemon into quarters, removing any pips or white pith. Cook in a large saucepan of boiling water for 5 minutes, then drain them and put the lemon quarters in a bowl of cold water and leave to soak for an hour.

Mix the sugar, salt and the measured water in a saucepan and put on the heat to dissolve. Drain the lemon quarters and add to the pan, bring them to the boil and then turn down the heat and let them simmer until the skins are tender, which should take about 20 minutes. Remove the lemons to a Kilner jar or similar and then reduce the syrup a little by letting it bubble away over high heat on the hob for a while, and pour over the lemons in the jar. The lemons will be ready to use the following day, though obviously you can keep them in their liquid in the jar to be plundered whenever you want them.

And actually, since you're going to need about 2 lemons' worth for the sea bass below, you might well want to boost quantities for regular use.

**for the sea bass:**

| | |
|---|---|
| 1 sea bass, approx. 1kg, gutted and scaled | small bunch fresh parsley, chopped |
| 3 tablespoons olive oil | 1 small bunch fresh mint, chopped |
| 6–8 quarters preserved lemons | 1 tablespoon syrup from the lemons |
| | black pepper |

Score the sea bass, making about three slashes almost to the bone on each side of the fish. Brush the fish with the olive oil, taking care to paint the head and tail well, as those parts stick the most.

Chop the lemon pieces finely and put them in a bowl with the chopped parsley and mint, mix everything up with your fingers and then stuff the six slashes with the lemon-herb mixture. Any herby, lemony gunge that's left once you've done this can be put into the cavity of the fish.

Lay the fish on a piece of foil and drizzle with the syrup, and season with black pepper. Then when you are ready to cook, lay the fish (on the foil) straight on to a very hot barbecue. Cooking the fish on a piece of foil means that it doesn't stick to the grill bars and you can also manoeuvre the fish off the heat easily when it's ready. Cook the sea bass for about 15 minutes. That's to say, it takes this long on my barbecue – which has a lid – but if you're cooking on an open barbecue, you will probably need to turn the fish. Otherwise, you can wrap the fish entirely in foil – making a tightly sealed but baggy package – and sit it on a baking tray in a hot oven (about 200°C/gas mark 6) for about the same length of time.

Serves 4.

## SALMON KEBABS WITH POMEGRANATE MOLASSES AND HONEY

Salmon may not be the most refined fish in the sea, but it does have the advantage of being able to take just about anything you want to throw at it. This may not be the most positive way of putting it; there is a lot to be said for its juicy coral meatiness. Here, treacly pomegranate molasses, honey and soy pervade it with sour-sweet pungency; once grilled, it takes on a burnished, barbecued stickiness.

80ml pomegranate molasses
80ml good-quality runny honey
1 tablespoon soy sauce

500g salmon fillet, cubed (approx. 4cm square)

Whisk together the pomegranate molasses, honey and soy, and pour into a freezer bag. Add the salmon pieces, and tie the bag, expelling any air first, then marinate for at least an hour.

Soak some wooden skewers in water, and then thread about three cubes of salmon on to each skewer. Barbecue or grill the fish for 3–4 minutes each side.

Makes 5 skewers.

I tend to shunt these kebabs on to my barbecue, but you can just as easily blister them under the grill. Think green Thai curry without the sauce – and to be frank you could stay within the correct register and just as easily make up kebabs by using chunked chicken or whole tiger prawns instead.

2 small Thai green chillies, roughly chopped

6 spring onions, roughly chopped

bunch fresh coriander, roughly chopped

1 tablespoon Thai fish sauce

juice of 2 limes

1 x 400g tin coconut milk

pinch salt

1 teaspoon caster sugar

1kg salmon fillet, cut into large cubes

Put the chillies, spring onions and coriander in a food processor and blitz until finely chopped. Add the fish sauce, lime juice, coconut milk, salt and sugar, and purée again until you have a thick paste.

Put the salmon cubes into a freezer bag and pour in the coconut marinade. Squeeze out the air, seal the bag tightly and leave in the fridge for at least an hour.

Thread the salmon on to wooden skewers that have been soaked in water; roughly, you should get about three cubes of fish for each kebab.

Barbecue for about 5 minutes; it's hard for me to be specific since I don't know how hot you can get your barbecue. And I find about 3 minutes a side more or less does it under a hot grill.

Makes about 10 skewers.

# SEAFOOD LAKSA

I love a laksa, that noodly hot, sweet stew, somewhere between a soup and a curry. I know there are a lot of ingredients, but the cooking itself is not labour intensive. If you can't find little red Thai shallots, then just use the same number of spring onions, chopped roughly before being put into the processor for blitzing. You can presume, as always, that the fish stock is not intended to be made from boney scratch. The regular bouillon concentrate will do fine.

2 long red chillies, deseeded

2cm ginger, peeled

1 teaspoon shrimp paste

8 Thai shallots, peeled

1 teaspoon turmeric

2 tablespoons groundnut oil

1 x 400ml tin coconut milk

1 litre fish stock

1 lemongrass, cut into 3

1 teaspoon tamarind water

2 teaspoons sugar

2 tablespoons fish sauce

250g medium raw prawns

250g cleaned squid tubes

125g beansprouts

250g medium flat rice noodles

bunch of coriander, chopped

Put the chillies, ginger, shrimp paste, shallots and turmeric into a food processor and blitz to a paste. Heat the oil in a wide saucepan and tip the mixture in, frying gently to soften but not colour.

Add the coconut milk, fish stock, lemongrass, tamarind, sugar and fish sauce, and bring to the boil.

Butterfly the prawns by cutting halfway through the inside curve of each prawn so that they fan out. Cut the squid into bite-sized squares and score them in a hatch pattern, taking care not to cut them all the way through. Add the seafood to the laksa, and then soak the beansprouts for a few seconds in boiling water and the noodles for a little longer until they rehydrate. (Check the packet instructions for the noodles you are using.) When the prawns and squid are cooked, in about 5–10 minutes, add the beansprouts and noodles and take the pan off the heat.

Ladle into bowls, sprinkling some freshly chopped coriander on top.

Serves 4–6.

I first ate this sitting under a shade on a small, unpeopled Ibicencan beach bar a few summers ago, and just had to make it, or a version of it, myself once back. It's not what one
might automatically think of as Spanish food; the fish, the way it's prepared, as well as
the dill that's sprinkled on top remind me far more of northern European cooking. Still,
let's be realistic; the influx of Germans over the years (while it hasn't reached Mallorcan
levels of teutonisation) must account for its inclusion on the menu in the first place.

But derivation is of academic interest only. This is wonderful: light and refreshing and very, very easy to put together. It does, however, need to be cooked, if that's the
word, at the last minute; any more than 10 minutes' steeping and the lime juice denatures
and bleaches the salmon too much. Though if the idea of uncooked salmon spooks you
– though why? – you can turn the slices quickly in a hot, oilless frying pan first.

If you get the salmon from a fishmonger, ask for it to be sliced like smoked
salmon; otherwise just buy escalopes. I have to say, though, that I love it unmarinaded:
that's to say, left fleshily raw and coral still; you don't have to change anything about the
way you prepare it, you just take it to the table the minute everything's on the plate.

Dill is one of those herbs which you love or detest; feel free to substitute chives
or coriander or, indeed, leave it herbless.

| | |
|---|---|
| juice of 1 lime | 325g salmon, sliced very thin |
| 1 x 15ml tablespoon extra virgin | 6 baby gherkins |
| olive oil | 4 tablespoons capers |
| Maldon salt | fresh dill for sprinkling over |
| white pepper, only if you have it to hand | |

Squeeze the lime juice into a jug and fork in the the oil, salt and pepper. Using a pair of
scissors, cut the salmon pieces into rough raggedy strips and arrange them on a large
plate or a couple of plates. Pour the lime juice mixture over, cut the baby gherkins into
slender slices lengthways and toss them, along with the capers, on top.

Sprinkle with dill and take to the table. Some Northern impulse in me makes me
want to prompt you to eat it with pumpernickel. But buttered brown bread is fine: or (as
I, to be frank, most often eat it), go pure and carbohydrate-free and just put a green salad
on the table alongside.

Serves 4.

There is something about fresh, really fresh, grilled sardines that reminds me instantly of those long holiday lunches in rented summer houses abroad. But if neither sardines, nor a fishmonger to fillet them, are available, know that this lemon salsa is terrific with any fish – and indeed most meats. Most often I use mint in this; sometimes I replace it with coriander: occasionally I use both, in tandem. I don't think there's a way this could taste bad. Try it with a little bit of chopped tarragon alongside some summery-grilled chicken.

**24 medium sardines (boned)**

**for the salsa:**
**2 lemons**
**1 large or 2 small red onions**

**small bunch fresh parsley**
**small bunch fresh mint (or coriander)**
**125ml extra virgin olive oil**
**juice of half a lemon**
**Maldon salt and black pepper**

Preheat the grill (or a barbecue) to the hottest it will go.

Peel the lemons following the instructions for the lemony prawn salad on page 96, then chop them roughly and chuck them in a bowl. Now chop the red onion, parsley and mint (or coriander) either by hand or in the processor, being careful – please – not to turn them to mush.

Mix the oniony herby mixture with the chunks of lemon in the bowl and stir in the olive oil and lemon juice, salt and pepper. Sometimes, I have to say, I add some crumbled dried red chilli pepper (or a finely chopped fresh green or red chilli) as well.

Leave the salsa to macerate while you cook the sardines. When they're really fresh, they scarcely need much time: just blitz them under a hot grill, transfer them to a waiting plate, sprinkle with Maldon salt and take to the table with the summer-sharp lemon salsa in its bowl alongside.

Serves 6–8.

# PEPPER-SEARED TUNA

Those of my vintage may remember this dish from the eighties fondly as Tataki of Tuna: a log of ludicrously rubied fish, rolled in pepper, briefly seared and eaten finely sliced with shredded spring onions and twiggy strips of cucumber. Dunk in soy as you eat or go for the Vietnamese dipping sauce on page 75 to go with it, or simply make up a few blobs of sinus-clearing wasabi. And if you do have some wasabi to hand, you can use this for smearing over the tuna, before coating it with peppercorns, in place of the English mustard stipulated below.

**1 tablespoon sesame oil**

**1 teaspoon English mustard**

**3–4 tablespoons black peppercorns, crushed roughly in a pestle and mortar**

**500g sashimi-quality tuna fillet, cut in a log of even thickness at either end**

***to serve:***

**cucumber, cut into slender batons**

**a few spring onions, cut into short lengths and then into fine strips**

In a small bowl mix the oil and mustard, and use a pastry brush to paint it on the tuna. Roll the tuna in the crushed peppercorns so that the long sides of the log are covered, but the ends are not.

Heat a dry frying pan until it's very hot and cook the tuna on all the long sides, searing the fish to about 3mm in a circle around the edge. You'll be able to see how much of it's cooked, because the ruby flesh will turn brown and the depth of the ring, if you see what I mean, will be evident from the uncoated round ends. Take out of the pan immediately and cool on a plate.

With a sharp knife cut into the finest slices you can and serve with the cucumber and spring onions and soy, dipping sauce, wasabi, as you please.

Serves 8 as a starter.

I'm on dangerous ground. Let me admit this straightaway. The recipe I'm about to give you is, purportedly, from Kerala – and have I ever been there? Well, I dream. And my excuse is, making this food is my way of dreaming. But even had I been there I wouldn't be making any straight-faced claims for the ensuing recipe's authenticity. One always has to be honest, and I'm never going to be other than a greedy girl with a wide-ranging appetite: what I can never be is Keralan.

But I have eaten Keralan food, cooked by those who actually come from there and, being a complete cookbook junkie, have the titles to slaver over in the comfort of my own home. And I love the food from this region. It is such a refined cuisine, in the best sense: the spices are used delicately to produce food that is aromatic rather than cough-inducingly hot; the scents of coconut, lime, coriander, pervade rather than invade.

This tamarind-tangy curry, the fragrant lemoniness of the rice, make for a perfect dinner on a hot night; light enough not to knock you out, but spiced enough to prompt a heat-drowsy appetite. And it is such gloriously easy food to make. In summer, particularly, that counts.

You can easily use any fish, chopped into meaty chunks for the curry itself (I've even gone hideously inappropriately for salmon in my time), though I tend to use whatever firm white fish I can lay my hands on; or just replace the fish with juicy, peeled uncooked prawns.

I've given a choice of amount for the tamarind paste: go by taste; it's up to you how evocatively pungent you want this. I happen to have a sour, rather than a sweet tooth, and this is where I indulge it. And I always keep a bottle of Benedicta's Touch of Taste fish bouillon concentrate in the house (which I buy from the supermarket, along with the tamarind paste), but you could crumble in half a fish stock cube if you prefer.

| | |
|---|---|
| **1.25kg firm white fish** | **2 long red chillies** |
| **salt** | **4cm piece fresh ginger** |
| **2 teaspoons turmeric** | **pinch ground cumin** |
| **1 tablespoon vegetable oil** | **1 x 400ml tin coconut milk** |
| **2 medium onions, halved and cut into** | **1–2 tablespoons concentrated tamarind** |
| **fine half-moons** | **1 tablespoon liquid fish stock** |

Cut the fish into bite-sized chunks, put them into a large bowl, and rub with a little salt and 1 teaspoon turmeric. Heat the oil in a large, shallow pan and peel and tip in your fine half-moons of onion; sprinkle them with a little salt to stop them browning and then cook, stirring, until they've softened; this should take scarcely 5 minutes.

Cut the whole, unseeded chillies into thin slices across (although if you really don't want this at all hot, you can deseed and then just chop them) and then toss them into the pan of softened onions. Peel the ginger and slice it, then cut the slices into strawlike strips and add them, too, along with the remaining teaspoon of turmeric and the cumin. Fry them with the onions for a few minutes.

Pour the tin of coconut milk into a measuring jug and add a tablespoon of tamarind paste and the fish stock, using boiling water from the kettle to bring the liquid up to the litre mark. Pour it into the pan, stirring it in to make the delicate curry sauce. Taste and add more tamarind paste if you want to. And actually you can do all this hours in advance if it helps.

When you are absolutely ready to eat, add the fish to the hot sauce and heat for a couple of minutes until it's cooked through, but still tender.

Serves 4–6.

# LEMON RICE

As you can – almost – see from the picture (on the previous page) this is a beautiful match for the Keralan fish curry. But all you need to know is that it tastes as wonderful. This way of cooking rice is very low stress, and the rice will keep, with a lid firmly clamped on it, without going sticky or overcooked for quite a while, so you don't need to live by the skin of your teeth.

**1 tablespoon vegetable oil**
**250g basmati rice**
**half teaspoon turmeric**
**half teaspoon dried mint**

**juice and zest of 1 lemon**
**approx. 500ml water**
**half teaspoon salt (or more to taste)**
**1 tablespoon black mustard seeds**

Choose a saucepan with a close-fitting lid, and heat the oil gently before adding the rice. Stir it around to get a good coating of oil and add the turmeric and mint, stirring to mix. Squeeze in the lemon juice (reserving the zest) and add the water, so that it covers the rice by a good couple of centimetres. Stir in the salt, put the lid on tightly, bring it to the boil, then reduce to a simmer and continue cooking very gently (on a heat diffuser if you've got one) with the lid on until all the water has been absorbed. This should take about 15 minutes. And if, when the rice has cooked, the pan is still a bit waterlogged, take it off the heat and replace the lid with a tea towel draped over to absorb the remaining water. It will sit quite happily like this if you need it to for about 30 minutes or even longer, and then you can fluff it with a fork, season it with some more salt if it needs it, and then turn the rice out into a bowl.

While the rice is cooking, toast the mustard seeds by heating them for a couple of minutes in a dry frying pan, then set aside. When you've turned the rice into its bowl, sprinkle these, along with the grated lemon zest, on top.

Serves 4–6.

Tuna is really the fish equivalent of steak and, in truth, you are eating it here as if it were beef, with a Japanese-mustardy beurre blanc. You can grill the tuna, fry it, cook it on the barbecue, as you please, but whichever method you use, make sure you cook it only briefly; you don't want the tuna to lose its melting Carpaccio-red interior completely.

**2 tablespoons white wine vinegar**
**150ml white wine**
**2 shallots, finely chopped**
**1 heaped teaspoon wasabi paste**
**1 tablespoon dark soy sauce or tamari**

**250g unsalted butter, cold and diced into**
  **1cm cubes**
**salt and pepper**
**1 bunch fresh coriander, chopped**
**6 tuna fillets, approx. 150g each**

Heat the grill for the tuna while you get on with the sauce.

Put the vinegar, wine and shallots into a small saucepan, and simmer to reduce the liquid to 1–2 tablespoons. Strain this reduction, and put it back into the pan adding the wasabi and soy. Then over a very gentle heat, whisk in cubes of cold butter, one at a time, so that the sauce emulsifies. Be careful that the sauce doesn't boil as it will split; just go slowly so that each cube of butter is absorbed before the next one goes in, though once most of the butter's in, you can actually add a couple at a time.

When all the butter is whisked in, check the seasoning and add the chopped coriander.

Quickly grill the tuna and serve the coriander-flecked butter sauce in a jug, or bowl with a spoon in it, alongside. All you need to eat it with is a bowlful of steamed, leggy tender-stem broccoli.

Serves 6.

## RED MULLET WITH SWEET AND SOUR SHREDDED SALAD

We are in rose-tinted heaven here: the pink glint of the red mullet's skin flashes like a Barbie-mermaid's tail against a salad of shredded pawpaw, red chilli pepper, carrot and spring onions, sprinkled pinkly with chopped, raw red-skinned peanuts.

If you can't get hold of green pawpaw, I wouldn't worry: most pawpaws are sold so unripe that you can slice them up as they are. Only when they are properly, juicily, coral are they unusable here.

There is something about the spiky, spicy sourness of the lime and fish-sauce dressed salad, and its nutty crunchiness, that makes this intensely refreshing and, if I may say it, unfishily inviting. It's also a doddle to make, and I can tell you now you will be making it again and again, no question.

**2 small red mullet, either whole or filleted, with the skin left on**

**for the salad:**
**4 tablespoons Thai fish sauce**
**juice of 1 lime**
**1 teaspoon caster sugar**
**50g raw peanuts in their red husks, chopped**

**50g (or a quarter) green pawpaw, finely julienned**
**2 small carrots, peeled and finely julienned**
**2 spring onions, finely julienned**
**small bunch fresh coriander, chopped**
**1 long red chilli, deseeded and finely julienned**

Slash the fish if they are whole, or lay the fillets on some foil, and either barbecue, or cook the fish in a hot oven at 200°C/gas mark 6 for about 10 minutes. Remove to a serving plate.

Combine all of the ingredients for the salad and scatter and pour it over the cooked fish if they are whole. If you are using fillets, spread a bed of dressing and lay the fillets on top.

Serves 2.

You can take the girl out of the eighties, but you can't quite take the eighties out of the girl. Far be it from me to call for a return to la nouvelle cuisine, but this is a chunky *hommage* to the seafood medleys of yore. You don't have to adhere to the three-fish rule if you don't want to; you don't even need to use the fish I specify. Any fish will do here, but certainly the coral, deep pink and white-ish mixture specified looks, and tastes, wonderful.

**2 salmon fillets, approx. 150g each**
**2 swordfish fillets, approx. 150g each**
**2 tuna fillets, approx. 150g each**
**3 tablespoons olive oil for frying**

*for the three herb sauce:*
**125ml extra virgin olive oil**

**zest of 1 lemon, juice of half**
**3 tablespoons fresh parsley, chopped**
**2 tablespoons capers preserved in**
**vinegar, drained but not rinsed**
**half teaspoon dried oregano**
**half teaspoon dried mint**
**salt and pepper**

Make your herb sauce by combining everything in a bowl, whisking it together rather like a salad dressing. Leave it to macerate for at least 15 minutes for the flavours to develop.

Cut each fillet of fish into three pieces so that you have longish strips. Fry them in the olive oil beginning with the salmon as it will need the longest, then the swordfish and finally the tuna.

Arrange them on a large flat plate so that the different fish intermingle, and drizzle the herb sauce over the top. Serve the remaining sauce in a bowl alongside.

Serves 6–8.

The dressing for this works along the same principle as the dressing for the squid salad on page 19: you peel the lemon and purée it, this time with spring onion, garlic and oil, in the processor. The cos lettuce is torn into bite-sized chunks and tossed in this thick lemony dressing; the prawns are quickly fried, laid hot on top and sprinkled with chives. This is one of my favourite summer lunches, or indeed suppers, of all time. I don't normally portion food up individually, but this is how I make this: one person, one plate.

**1 lemon**
**2 cloves garlic**
**1 spring onion, roughly chopped**
**2 tablespoons groundnut oil**
**5 tablespoons olive oil**

**3 cos lettuce hearts, or 1 large cos lettuce**
**375g medium raw prawns, shelled and deveined**
**small bunch chives, chopped**

Peel the lemon by cutting the tops and bottoms off then sit it upright on one end, and cut away the zest and pith from top to bottom with a sharp knife, turning it with your non-cutting hand as you go. Chop it roughly and put it in the processor with one of the cloves of garlic and the spring onion and blitz. Open, scrape down, then stick the lid back on and, with the motor running, pour the groundnut oil and 3 tablespoons of the olive oil down the funnel into the processor. Roughly tear the cos lettuce into pieces, toss with this dressing and divide between two large plates.

Heat the remaining olive oil in a large frying pan and gently heat the second garlic clove until lightly golden to infuse the oil. Take out the garlic clove and add the prawns to the pan. Cook for 5–6 minutes until cooked through and no longer glassy in the middle. Spoon them over the dressed salad leaves, being scrupulously fair as to how you divide them (if there's an odd number, I'd wolf it down as you stand by the stove) and sprinkle over the chopped chives.

Serves 2.

# SEARED MUSTARD-COATED SALMON

This is an incredibly easy, incredibly quick main course to go with the beetroot salad on page 54 and the Hasselback potatoes on page 151. There is nothing intrinsically Scandinavian about it, but the flavours of this soft-fleshed fish dredged in sweet mustard are certainly borrowed from the Swedish palate. The sweet heat evokes the almost honeyed vinegariness of certain herring marinades, or that sauce which goes with gravadlax, but this way sharpens it, gives it a modern, less cloying edge. The sugar in which the salmon pieces are dredged helps an almost caramelly crust to form, but the acrid heat of the mustard powder undercuts any sweetness.

All I ask is that you don't dredge the fish until the absolute moment you want to cook it, otherwise the coating will make it claggy rather than crusty.

**6 x 200g skinless salmon fillets**
**1–2 tablespoons olive oil**
**2 scant tablespoons caster sugar**

**2 heaped tablespoons English mustard powder**

Put a frying pan on the heat with a tablespoonful of oil in it. I've specified olive oil, but don't use the good – extra virgin – stuff here; at this heat, it would be a complete waste.

Mix half the sugar and half the mustard powder on a plate and dunk in half of the fish fillets, first one side and then the other. Cook them on a medium to high heat – you want to hear the pan sizzle – for about 3 minutes a side.

Remove to a warmed plate and do an action replay with the remaining the oil, fish, sugar and mustard powder. The salmon should be a burnished brown without, juicily coral within. Remember, too, that the fish will continue to cook as it waits for a few minutes on the plate before anyone starts to eat it.

Serves 6.

# SEA BASS WITH SAFFRON, SHERRY AND PINE NUTS

This is another fabulously easy recipe – and you can be totally relaxed about it. That's to say, consider it simply a guide: use other fish fillets if you like, or indeed substitute chicken breasts; just remember they'll need much longer cooking and therefore probably more liquid. I reckon that the kilo of fish stipulated below should be about two medium-sized bass, filleted. I then cut each fillet in half or thirds, so that you'll have either eight or twelve smaller slices to cook. I love this with a small pile of plain white basmati rice and a contrasting bowlful of dark, muddy lentils.

**1kg fillets sea bass, skinned**
**Maldon salt**
**2 tablespoons sultanas**
**good pinch saffron strands**

**4 tablespoons Amontillado sherry**
**3 tablespoons pine nuts**
**125ml water**

Cut the fish into smaller pieces, however you want, and sprinkle lightly with salt. Put the sultanas in a bowl, strew with the saffron, warm up the sherry and pour it over. Put a thick-bottomed frying pan on the heat and toss the pine nuts in it until they take on a deep gold colour and give off their waxy aromatic scent. Pour on to a plate and put on one side. Pour the sultanas in their saffroned sherry into the emptied-out pan and add the water, then put it back on the heat and let it come to a simmer, then add the fish fillets, or as many as will fit in one layer; add more water if they are not more or less submerged. After about a minute's simmering, turn them over with a couple of spatulas. They cook very quickly and if you leave it too long, they'll flake as you turn them. Give them another minute or so on the second side and remove to a waiting plate. Continue till you've used up all the fish, adding more water as necessary. When you've finished, use the spatula to remove as many sultanas as you can to the cooked fish on the plate, then turn the heat under the frying pan to high and let the sherry-saffron juices reduce till you have a just-liquid yellow syrup. Pour this over the fish, then scatter over the toasted pine nuts. And that's all there is to it.

Serves 6–8.

MEAT

# PORCHETTA

This is a domestic take on the Italian marketplace staple of roast suckling pig, and quite my favourite thing to eat in Italy. I've specified pork shoulder, but really you can get any cut of pork you want: the important thing is that it's opened out to form a roughly oblong slab or sheet, which you then smear with onion, fennel seeds, rosemary, bay leaves, ground cloves and garlic, then you roll it up so that the flavourings snake their way through the whole of the joint. Tie it with string, roast it for a good long time then, once it's out of the oven, leave it till it's still just warm then slice it thickly and wodge it into buns. Of course you can just carve it and eat it more sedately with knife and fork, but for the echt experience, pretty well unbeatable, you need to taste this aromatic, slow-cooked pork in sandwich form at least once. I tend to keep within the authentic register and get small, individual ciabatta rolls, but even in thick slices of white English bread it's dreamy. But don't use a plastic sliced loaf, which will go too pappy, and avoid baguettes: that robust crunch is not what we're going for here.

**2kg neck end pork shoulder, derinded, boned and butterflied**
**3 tablespoons olive oil**
**1 large onion, chopped**
**3 cloves garlic, finely chopped**
**2 tablespoons fennel seeds**

**2 large sprigs fresh rosemary, finely chopped**
**4 fresh bay leaves, finely chopped**
**1 teaspoon ground cloves**
**1 teaspoon salt**
**8 black peppercorns, coarsely crushed**
**8–10 or so ciabatta buns**

Lay the pork out on a chopping board and cover with clingfilm. Using either a rolling pin or meat mallet pound the meat to an even 3cm thickness or as near as you can get. Heat 2 tablespoons of the oil in a frying pan and cook the onion for a few minutes until it's beginning to soften. Add half the garlic, half the fennel seeds, all the rosemary and bay leaves, half the ground cloves, the salt and pepper, and cook for a minute more, then transfer to a plate and leave it to cool.

Spread this cooled mixture over the pork, rubbing it in well, then roll up the pork tightly and secure at regular intervals with string. If you're as cack-handed as I am, you might find it helpful to have someone to keep a steady finger on the string as you tie it, but it's not impossible single-handed.

Mix together the remaining garlic, fennel and ground cloves with the remaining olive oil. Rub this over the surface of the pork. Loosely cover with clingfilm and leave to steep in the fridge overnight or for 24 hours. But do remember to take it out of the fridge a good 40 minutes before you start cooking as the meat has to be at room temperature when it goes into the oven.

So, preheat the oven to 180°C/gas mark 4, and put the pork in a roasting tin and cook for 4 hours. It may need covering towards the end of the cooking time, so look at it after about 3 – if it looks as if it's beginning to blacken too much (a little bit of herby burning just adds to the depth of flavour), tent it loosely with foil for the last hour.

Remove from the oven and leave, uncovered, for an hour or so before slicing it, stuffing it into whatever rolls or bread you're using, then just sink your teeth into these melting-bellied, dangerously compulsive bulging buns.

Fills 8–10 buns.

For all that we try and put the blame on the Hawaiians, there does seem to me to be something ineffably, if embarrassingly, English about the combination of ham and pineapple. I do not want to eat them together on my pizza, but like this, they justify the pairing. You may smirk, but this is not intended as an ironic exercise in gastro-rehabilitation here. Food, like life, has to be real, and this tastes really good. For all my robust internationalism – motto: if it tastes good, eat it – I do think that in the few warm weeks given to us, one wants food that reminds one of past summers, long ago ones, real or wistfully imagined. For me this means cold ham. Not that this is by any means an exclusively summer notion: when it's cold out, eat the gammon – as ham should properly be called once it's cooked – hot, but keep this accompaniment of sunny pineapple relish or salsa, however you want to think of it. You can use either mint or coriander in the pineapple relish: coriander takes it definitively into the domain of the salsa; mint gives it a cooling, English air. You choose. And if you want to mix the relish in the processor, then roughly chop everything, put the herbs and onions in and blitz first, then add the pineapple and lime juice and pulse.

These days, I find that you don't need to soak ham before cooking it, but if you have any reason to believe you've got a piece of extremely salty ham in front of you, either sit it in a sinkful of cold water overnight or, when you cook it, put it in a panful of cold water, bring it to the boil then chuck out the water and proceed as below.

**1 x 2.5–3kg mild cure gammon joint**
**1 x 1 litre carton pineapple juice**
**1 ripe pineapple**
**5 spring onions, trimmed, halved**
 **then finely sliced**
**juice of 1 lime**

**4 tablespoons chopped fresh coriander or**
 **6 tablespoons chopped fresh mint**
**1 green chilli, deseeded roughly and**
 **finely chopped**
**salt**

To cook the gammon, put the joint in a pan, pour over the pineapple juice and then add cold water to cover well. Put the pan on to boil, then turn down and cook at a simmer for 50 minutes per kg then, once it's cooked, let it sit and cool in the liquid. Or eat it straightaway, keeping the liquid so that any leftovers can cool in it afterwards; this is the best way of making sure the gammon doesn't dry out as it cools.

To make the relish, slice the pineapple, halve the slices then cut away the core and the skin and chop the fruit finely. Squeeze the pieces of skin over the bowl to catch any juices going, then stir in the onions, lime juice, herbs and chilli and add salt to taste, remembering that the ham will be fairly salty.

Serves 8.

Until I made these, I thought they were best eaten in Chinese restaurants. But there is just something about having a huge pile of these at home that has made me rethink entirely. Sticky with honey, but salty sharp with soy and rice wine vinegar, aromatically resonant with ginger, cinnamon, star anise and five-spice powder and eaten with a fresh and spiky scattering of chilli and spring onions, these are fabulous to pick at languorously and messily, the supreme reward for unchecked greed. They are also wonderful made with shop-bought Chinese sweet chilli sauce (I use about 6 tablespoons of the stuff) in the place of the fresh chopped chilli and honey.

You can often find sheets of spare ribs at the supermarket, or ask your butcher to cut them for you.

**16 pork spare ribs**

*for the marinade:*
**4 tablespoons rice wine vinegar**
**3 tablespoons soy sauce**
**2 red chillies, roughly chopped**
**5cm piece fresh ginger, peeled and cut**
    **into thin slices**
**2 tablespoons runny honey**
**2 star anise**
**1 stick cinnamon, broken into pieces**
**1 teaspoon sesame oil**

**2 tablespoons groundnut oil**
**4 spring onions, roughly chopped**

*to cook:*
**2 teaspoons five-spice powder**
**2 tablespoons runny honey**

*to serve:*
**2 red or green chillies, deseeded or**
    **not to taste, finely chopped**
**2 spring onions, finely chopped, or a**
    **small bunch of coriander, chopped**

Put the ribs into a large plastic bag and add all the marinade ingredients, tie a knot and squidge everything around well. Ideally leave in a fridge overnight, or for at least a couple of hours in a cool place somewhere in the kitchen.

Preheat the oven to 200°C/gas mark 6.

Let the marinated ribs come to room temperature, and pour the whole contents of the bag into a roasting tin. Cover tightly with foil and put the tin in the oven for 1 hour.

Take the foil off the roasting tin and sprinkle over the five-spice powder and spoon over the amber honey. Put the ribs back in the oven for another 30 minutes, take them out half way through and turn them over before returning them to become stickily glazed on the underside. Watch that they don't catch: they may only need another 10 minutes to become crispy and glossily brown.

Take them out of their tin, arrange on a large plate and scatter over the chopped chilli and spring onion or coriander.

Serves 4–5.

# LOMO DE ORZA

*Lomo* is pork loin and the *orza* is the terracotta dish in which it's traditionally marinated. I found this recipe in Penelope Casas' *Tapas: The Little Dishes of Spain*, and I can't tell you how bowled over I was by it. You need to start it the day before you want to eat it, but in a way that makes it easier. But believe me, even if it were harder to make it would be worth it. The marinade it's steeped in, *after* it's fried, makes it meltingly tender and flavoursome without being heavy scented. I get the butcher to slice the pork loin leaving the fat on, as that's what gives this its wonderful flavour, but if you're buying the meat from the supermarket just get any piece of loin you can find and slice it thickly yourself. Simply served with a salad and some baked potatoes, it makes a wonderful low-key, evocatively sunny Saturday lunch at any time of the year.

**625g boneless pork loin, cut into
  2.5cm slices
Maldon salt and black pepper
250ml plus 2 tablespoons olive oil
juice of half a lemon**

**quarter of a teaspoon dried thyme
3–4 sprigs fresh rosemary, needles
  finely chopped
4 cloves garlic, peeled and crushed**

Season the pork with salt and pepper, and brown in a pan with the 2 tablespoons of oil. Lower the heat once the meat has a good colour and cook for a further 15 minutes or until the pork is cooked through but still juicy.

Put the meat into a shallow dish – preferably earthenware – big enough to hold the pork all in one layer, and pour over the remaining olive oil, along with the juices from the pan. Add the remaining ingredients and make sure the meat is immersed in the marinade. Cover with foil and leave overnight at room temperature. If it's very hot, though, it might be better off in the fridge.

When you are ready to eat, cut the meat at a diagonal (and if it's been in the fridge take it out a good 20 minutes beforehand so it isn't unyieldingly cold). Arrange the slices on a large plate and spoon over some of the oily marinade. Fabulous.

Serves 4–6.

# LAMB KEBABS

You could use any of the marinades for the barbecued loins on page 118, but this is how I most often make kebabs, either to go with the za'atar chicken on page 134 or instead of, to go with the accompanying fattoush. The nutty, deeply resonant thyme mixture is just perfect with the sweet cubes of lamb.

**500g lean lamb, cubed**

**125ml olive oil**

**2 cloves garlic, bruised**

*for the marinade:*

**2 tablespoons za'atar**

**juice of 1 lemon, plus skins thrown in**

**1 medium onion, quartered**

Put the cubed lamb in a large freezer bag, then add all the marinade ingredients. Tie a knot, making sure any air is expelled first, then squeeze the bag about a bit to let the marinade squelch over the lamb. Leave this in the fridge overnight (or for up to a couple of days) or, out of the fridge in some cool place in the kitchen, for at least a couple of hours.

Let the meat come to room temperature, and soak about ten bamboo skewers in water for about half an hour.

Either heat a grill, or a griddle (or the barbecue of course), then thread three or four pieces of meat on to each skewer and slap on the heat.

These are also wonderful with a cooling mound of the cacık on page 57.

Makes about 10 skewers.

This bulgar wheat salad is loosely based on tabbouleh, only using coriander in place of the parsley, lime in place of the lemon and omitting the tomatoes and adding the chilli and some raw, diced courgettes. Coriander is so much more headily aromatic than parsley that I've made the ratio to herb and grain skewed differently from traditional tabbouleh: that's to say, this is a herb-flecked grainy salad, rather than a herb salad into which a few grains have been tossed. Because the bulgar wheat is so strongly flavoured and aromatic you can leave the lamb as it is: no marinade, no nothing, just sweet and pink and warm against the green-flecked cracked wheat. If you want to serve the lamb on top of the salad, I find that two loins of lamb are plenty, but if you want to serve the meat on a separate plate, then I'd go for three. This may sound mad, but really it does seem to make a difference to how people eat.

250g bulgar wheat

2-3 lamb loins, approx. 300g each

very large bunch fresh coriander, weight of leaves, without stalks, approx. 50g

large bunch fresh mint, weight of leaves, without stalks, approx. 40g

6–8 spring onions

1 fresh green chilli

2 small or 1 medium courgette

juice of 4–5 limes

8 tablespoons olive oil

salt and pepper

Following the packet instructions, cover the bulgar wheat with water and leave to steep as directed.

Either on a griddle or in a frying pan, sear the lamb over high heat, and then turn down and let cook for about 10 minutes, by which time the meat should still be a soft, velvet pink within. When cooked, set aside until the salad is ready; you want the lamb warm rather than hot, in any case.

Now back to the salad. Chop the coriander and mint. If you promise not to leave it on for long, you can use the processor. Avoid reducing the herbs to wet mush: it's better to have the leaves left relatively large. Finely slice the spring onions and deseed the chilli and chop it very finely, too. Take half the courgette and peel it and dice it into very small pieces.

Drain the bulgar wheat in a sieve when it tastes tender and push and squeeze as much water out as possible. Pour over the juice of 4 limes and all the olive oil. Add salt and pepper and toss well, either with your hands or a couple of forks. Reserve a small handful of the chopped coriander and mint and throw the remainder of the chopped herbs, chilli, spring onions and courgette into the dressed bulgar wheat and mix deftly. Taste to see if you need more lime juice (or indeed anything else). Arrange on the biggest dish you can find and then thinly slice the lamb and place it on top, in the centre. Get the vegetable peeler and shave thin slices from the remaining courgette and scatter these, along with the handful of reserved herbs, on top.

Serves 8.

Having just come back from Rome, I can honestly say that there is nothing in this world that can match an Italian *fritto*. The joy of these, particularly, is that they are wonderful eaten cold as well, their pink juiciness trapped within their eggy parmesan coating. If you don't have any stale bread to hand for making the breadcrumbs, then just split open some pitta breads, leave them a short while – even half an hour will do – to dry out and then tear them up and blitz them in a processor.

**10 lamb chop cutlets with bone in**
**175g fresh white breadcrumbs or 3 pitta breads, processed**

**10g grated parmesan**
**2 eggs, beaten with salt and pepper**
**olive oil (not extra virgin) for frying**

Remove the thick layer of fat from around the edge of each little chop, either by tearing it off by hand, or with a pair of scissors. Be careful not to lose the shape of the chop, though, or it will fall to pieces on frying.

Layer the chops between two sheets of clingfilm, and beat them vigorously with a mallet or rolling pin so that they are flattened a little.

Then, in a wide, shallow bowl, combine the breadcrumbs and parmesan, and put the seasoned eggs in another bowl.

Pour some olive oil into a frying pan, to come about 1cm deep, and put it on the heat. Dip the lamb chops first in the eggy mixture and then press them well in the cheese and breadcrumbs before frying them in the hot oil. Cook the chops for about 3 minutes each side: they should be a deep golden brown and crunchy outside, within a still tender pink.

Eat them as they are, left to get to room temperature or even cold: there is no way these are anything less than compulsively delicious.

Serves 4.

The authentically Middle-Eastern way of doing this would be to marinate cubes of lamb and then make fat spears of grilled kebabs (and see page 109, above). But I use lamb cutlets, small and sweet and plump fleshed, and just eat them like kebabs, without cutlery, biting the flesh off the sharp little curved bones. Four hours is fine for marinating purposes, but if it makes life easier to get the lamb in its marinade the evening before, do.

This is a fantastically low-effort recipe: your most strenuous activity is peeling the garlic. And if it helps you feel relaxed, too, you can fry them in advance and serve them at room temperature. If you've got a ridged grill or frying pan use that to show them off at their charcoal-striped, impressive best, but an ordinary oven-bound grill or unfancy frying pan will do. Obviously, a barbecue would be wonderful; the yoghurt so tenderises the meat that however searing the heat, they just cannot dry up.

| | |
|---|---|
| **1 x 450–500g pot Greek yoghurt** | **1 teaspoon Maldon salt** |
| **1 tablespoon ground cumin** | **20 lamb cutlets** |
| **1 large onion** | **groundnut oil (optional)** |
| **1 head garlic** | |

Empty the yoghurt pot into a large shallow dish (it has to be big enough to fit all the lamb chops later, or use two) and then stir in the cumin. Peel and roughly chop the onion and add it. Break the head of garlic into cloves, peel them and squash them slightly just by pressing on them with the flat of a heavyish knife, then stir them into the yoghurt along with the salt. Then arrange the lamb cutlets and give a good slow stir, spooning the yoghurt over them, so that all the meat is coated with the marinade. You might think at first that this won't be possible and that you haven't got anywhere near enough yoghurt, but you want them only barely masked by the marinade, not deeply immersed in it.

Cover the dish or dishes with clingfilm and put in the fridge (or, if the weather isn't sweltering, in a cool place) for at least 4 hours.

When you want to eat, put a ridged grill pan or whatever on the hob and heat up (if you're using an ordinary frying pan, add a little oil) then take the lamb cutlets out of the marinade. Wipe them with some kitchen towel, but you don't need to dry them obsessively. Then just fry them for a few minutes each side, so that they're cooked as much or as little as you like them, and then arrange on a big plate or, better still, a couple of big plates (saves passing them up and down the table) and serve hot, warm or cold.

I love these with the moutabal on page 159, but I'm not fussy: a bowlful of the Greek Salad on page 62 would be fabulous too.

Serves 6–8.

By mint salsa, I mean something along the lines of an Italian salsa verde, but with that greenness in the main provided by finely chopped mint. We've grown to think there's something shameful in mint sauce, as if in cooking lamb the only worthy flavourings or accompaniments could be garlic and rosemary. Now, I still love mint sauce the way my mother made it, finely chopping the herb, then stirring in sugar and vinegar; this new-age take on it attempts to preserve what was so wonderful about it, the fresh sprightliness and piquancy, but bring to it a more modulated, modern tone.

With the lamb and this sauce, I tend to make – and we all have our own lazily unthinking, push-button repertoire – the new season's roast vegetables on page 153. The sour astringency of the salsa, indeed, goes so well with the sweet nubbliness of the baby veg, that I sometimes leave the lamb out of the equation altogether: just bake the vegetables and drizzle the herbal, acerbic green oil over, adding perhaps some more freshly chopped mint on top.

**2 racks of lamb, approx. 8 cutlets on each rack**

**for the mint sauce:**
**30g fresh mint (or 2 supermarket packets)**
**30g fresh flat-leaf parsley**
**16 cornichons (baby gherkins)**

**4 teaspoons capers**
**200ml extra virgin olive oil**
**4 teaspoons white wine vinegar, or to taste**
**pinch caster sugar**
**ground black pepper**
**Maldon salt**

Preheat the oven to 210°C/gas mark 7. Make sure the lamb is out of the fridge and well on its way to becoming room temperature; if still fridge-cold when they go into the oven add about 7 minutes' extra cooking time.

Destalk the herbs and whizz them in a food processor until they are chopped, then add the cornichons and capers and whizz again. Pour the oil down the funnel, and then add the vinegar and sugar to taste, and season with the black pepper and the salt.

Score the lamb fat, by using a sharp knife to draw diagonal lines, this way and that, about a couple of centimetres apart and, using a pastry brush, paint the fat with a coating of the mint sauce, saving the rest to serve with the lamb. Arrange the racks in an intertwining arch, and put them into a tin and thence into the oven to roast for about 20 minutes, depending on size.

Serves 4–6.

# MOROCCAN ROAST LAMB

Or how to make yourself feel basked in exotic, perfume-heavy sunshine when all about you is spirit-wizeningly cold and grey. For me, Moroccan is, so far, just a state of mind. In my defence, the crucial flavouring here is the very Moroccan ras-el-hanout, a musky, amber-coloured spice mix, heady with rosebuds, cardamom, cinnamon, nutmeg, allspice, lavender, ginger, pepper, mace and, I'm not too modest to admit, nigella, which you can, if you're lucky, find at the supermarket now (or direct from Seasoned Pioneers on 0800 0682 348). But then again, crucial is a flexible term: in place of the smokily poetic ras-el-hanout, you can add to the garlic and oil below, a teaspoon of turmeric mixed with a tablespoonful each of ground coriander and cumin and a pinch each of ground cinnamon and cloves – a no less magical substitution, I promise you.

**1 leg of lamb, approx. 2.5kg**

**1–2 tablespoons ras-el-hanout**

**juice of 2 lemons**

**6 tablespoons olive oil**

**2 cloves garlic, minced**

**bunch fresh coriander, chopped**

Make incisions all over the leg of lamb, and then mix the ras-el-hanout with the lemon juice, oil, minced garlic and coriander. Using your fingers, push pinches of the mixture into the holes. Rub the remaining aromatic paste over the lamb and then put it into a large freezer bag, squeeze out any air and then tie it up and leave it to marinate in the fridge overnight, or for longer.

Preheat the oven to 200°C/gas mark 6, and take the lamb out of the fridge to come to room temperature.

Put the leg of lamb into a roasting pan, squeezing any marinade out of the bag over the meat. Roast the lamb for about an hour and a half, by which time it should be aromatically blackened on the outside, and still tender and pink within. Let the lamb rest once it comes out of the oven for at least 15 minutes, though I love this a good hour after it's come out of the oven.

I don't want to be too bossy about how you should eat this: that's to say, I feel the urge, but am trying to resist it. I love it with a bowlful of moutabal (see page 159) and another of Puy or other lentils and some mace-scented basmati rice. But perhaps my favourite way, is to slice it into straggly rags and put it on a plate alongside a bowl of cacık (see page 57) and a tangle of whole mint and parsley leaves stirred through with some fine half-moons of red onion and a squeeze of lemon juice, with some sheets of soft bread-wraps or pitta on the table, too, so that people can roll up or stuff their own loose, free-form sandwiches as they eat.

Serves 8.

It's not just that you can marinate this lamb one of three ways: to be frank you have a triple choice for cooking it, too; a hot grill or frying pan would serve no less well than a barbecue. In either matter, I leave the choice to you.

In all cases, the marinades should be enough for two 300g loins of lamb, which should be enough, carved thinly, for eight greedy people.

**for the redcurrant marinade:**

| | |
|---|---|
| 1 x 150g punnet redcurrants | 1 clove garlic |
| 1 red onion, chopped | generous grinding black pepper |
| juice of 1 large orange | 2 scant tablespoons chilli oil |

I got the idea for this back to front: that's to say, I knew – hot on the trail of my mint salsa, on page 115 – I wanted to eat a redcurrant salsa with the lamb; it then occurred to me that the fruit's intense acidity would serve to tenderise the meat as well. It does, and beautifully. In fact, I use it for marinating chops in fairly regularly now, whether I'm making the salsa to eat with them or not.

To make the marinade, just put all the above ingredients in the processor and blitz. Tip into a freezer bag, add the lamb loins and tie up, expelling any air first. Leave for at least an hour at room temperature or stash in the fridge overnight.

Cook the lamb loins whichever way you find easiest. The important thing is to make sure the meat's at room temperature before you start. And, since I love the meat really juicily pink within, I tend to give the loins no more than about 15–20 minutes' cooking; if they're very thin, less.

**for the redcurrant salsa:**

| | |
|---|---|
| 1 small red onion, chopped | small handful fresh mint |
| 150g redcurrants | zest of 1 orange |

Put the onion in the bowl of the food processor and then blitz until roughly chopped. Add the redcurrants and pulse till both onion and currants are chopped but not mush. Tip into a bowl, and chop the mint in the processor (or by hand) and add this into the onion and redcurrant mix. Grate in the zest of the orange and stir everything together to combine.

*for the yoghurt and mint marinade:*

250g Greek yoghurt

juice of half a lemon

2 tablespoons dried mint

2 tablespoons green (or any)
  peppercorns, bruised

2 cloves garlic, minced

3 tablespoons vegetable oil

Mix all the ingredients for the marinade together in a freezer bag and add the lamb loins. Marinate and cook as above. I tend to want to echo the flavours of the marinade in the accompaniment, by which I mean I usually make a bowlful of cacık (see page 57) to go with.

*for the cumin rub:*

3 cloves garlic, minced

3 tablespoons ground cumin

1 tablespoon Maldon salt, crushed

4 tablespoons olive oil

Mix the above ingredients into an aromatic paste and smear the lamb loins with this. Sit them on a plate, cover with clingfilm and leave for about an hour at room temperature or leave to steep overnight in the fridge. Barbecue, fry or grill the loins, leave to stand for a few minutes before slicing thinly and eat as you might the Moroccan roast lamb on page 117 or, indeed, any way you like.

Think hamburger, Middle-Eastern style. And if this isn't enough of a come-on, think again. I am mad for these pitta-sandwiches smeared with hummus and stuffed with red onion, mint, shredded lettuce and small mint-and-oregano flavoured lamb patties.

**for the patties:**
**50g bulgar wheat**
**500g lean lamb, minced**
**4 teaspoons dried mint**
**4 teaspoons dried oregano**
**1 clove garlic**
**zest of 1 lemon**
**olive oil for frying**

**for the sandwiches:**
**approx. 8 pitta breads**

**1 or so Little Gem lettuces, shredded**
**large bunch fresh mint, chopped**
**1 red onion, halved and sliced into very**
**  thin half-moons**
**1 x tub hummus (approx. 300g)**
**1 x tub Greek yoghurt (approx.**
**  300g)**
**approx. 1 teaspoon ground cumin**
**about 4 tomatoes**
**1 or 2 lemons**

Soak the bulgar wheat by covering it with boiling water and leaving it for 15 minutes in a small bowl.

Drain the bulgar thoroughly, pressing the water out in a sieve and put it in a bowl with the minced lamb. Add the dried mint and oregano, mince in the garlic (I just grate it with a fine microplane) and the lemon zest. Stir everything thoroughly and then form into small walnut-sized patties, then flatten them slightly between your hands and arrange them, as you go, on a clingfilmed baking sheet or plate and let them stand for 20 minutes in the fridge to firm up. If you want to, you can cover them with clingfilm, too, and leave them in the fridge for up to 6 hours before frying them. I get, by the way, about 34 patties out of this mixture.

Fry the patties in a little olive oil until cooked through, and a beautiful golden brown on both sides. These are little, so it shouldn't take too long: I'd reckon on about 4 minutes a side. The important thing is not to crowd the pan as you cook.

To make up your sandwiches, roughly proceed as follows. Toast or otherwise warm each pitta bread and cut a strip off one long side to open it, then stuff it with a salad of shredded lettuce, chopped mint and half-moons of red onion rings. Dollop into each gaping pitta (and you can do this before or after the salad stage actually) a couple of tablespoons of hummus mixed with 1 tablespoon Greek yoghurt and a pinch of ground cumin. Cram with four or five lamb patties, then squeeze in half a tomato roughly chopped and give a good spritz of lemon juice.

Makes about 8 bulging sandwiches.

# BLACK AND BLUE BEEF

'Black and blue' is the New York restaurateur's term for the way I like my steak cooked: charred on the outside, meltingly, quiveringly rare within. It is in the spirit of internationalism, and in deference to this year's World Cup, that I suggest this now Korean style, in a soy, ginger and garlic marinade, and then thinly sliced so that you end up with a plateful of spice-seared, ruby-fleshed rags, the whole both scorched and tender.

| | |
|---|---|
| **4 approx. 4cm-thick slices, cut from the top of the rump (approx. 1.5kg in weight)** | **3 garlic cloves, minced** |
| | **2.5cm fresh ginger, minced** |
| | **2 tablespoons sesame oil** |
| | **2 teaspoons caster sugar** |
| *for the marinade:* | **black pepper** |
| **5 tablespoons soy sauce** | **4 spring onions, roughly chopped** |

Put the steaks in a large freezer bag and add all the marinade ingredients. Tie the bag expelling any air, and squidge everything around before leaving in the fridge overnight (or even for a day or so), or for at least an hour at room temperature.

Grill on a viciously hot barbecue or on a griddle. I like to do not much more than blacken the outside (which means about 5 minutes per side) but you, of course, should cook this just as long as you like. Leave to stand for a few minutes before carving into thin slices.

I love to eat these red, savoury, straggly slices mounded on plain steamed rice, wodged into buns with a splodge of brown sauce or piled into the centre of a Chinese-pancake-thin soft flatbread, drizzled with some of the Vietnamese Dipping Sauce on page 75 and rolled up to form slaveringly dripping wraps.

Serves 4.

# STEAK WITH BARBECUE BUTTERS

This is the Euro-alternative to the Korean-flavoured steak above. I tend always to give people their own individual steaks when I make flavoured butters, simply because this is best with a retro-disc of herb-flecked butter sitting melting on each one.

Make up one or all of these butters as you want. The point about them is, you can leave them in their clingfilmed sausage shapes in the deep freeze, then slice off what you need when you want.

I love making them, not least because all that squidging and rolling makes me feel quite uncharacteristically brisk and competent. I normally avoid any sort of cooking where deftness is required, but somehow this does it all for you: no expertise is necessary at all.

To go with any of the butters below (or add your own flavourings as desired), cook rump, sirloin or fillet steaks and add a herbed medallion on each the minute you put them, hot, on the plate. I specify unsalted butter but require you to add salt. I promise you this does make sense: on the whole, unsalted butter is of a vastly superior quality; it's not the saltiness itself to which I object.

*for the bagna cauda butter:*
**1 x 50g tin anchovies**
**200g unsalted butter**
**125ml extra virgin olive oil**
**4 cloves garlic, minced**
**black pepper**

*for the lime and coriander butter:*
**40g fresh coriander**
**juice of 2 limes**
**200g unsalted butter**
**generous sprinkling Maldon salt**

*for the lemon and thyme butter:*
**10–15 sprigs fresh thyme**
**juice of 2 lemons**
**200g unsalted butter**
**generous sprinkling Maldon salt**

*for the blue cheese butter:*
**200g Roquefort cheese**
**200g unsalted butter**
**black pepper**

The method for all these butters is the same and relaxingly simple.

Purée all the ingredients for the butters in the processor; the butter should not be rock-solid cold, but it works better when it isn't very soft either. This makes things easy, actually, because it means you don't have to get the butter out of the fridge hours before using it. So you can either make this in advance and keep it all in the freezer before using it, or regard it as a quick, last-minute idea for pepping up the odd steak.

Now, forming the butter logs is easy enough; the hard thing is to explain it.

Tear off a sheet of clingfilm and lay it on the counter, longways, in front of you. Splodge out the processed mixture in the centre to form a rough sausage shape, but don't worry if all the splodges aren't connected. That's to say, they will all come together to form a log as you roll. Wrap the butter by covering it first with the top bit of clingfilm, that's to say, the bit that is above it, then cover it with the bit below. Twiddle the ends as if you were making a Christmas cracker then, working from the top of the counter and coming towards you, keep rolling the loose cracker shape and with each roll, a sausage shape will take form in front of you, the butter compressing together and turning into a fat round log. Either sit this sausagey butter log in the fridge or in the deep freeze. Let the frozen discs thaw a little before using, and sit a slice or two on top of each hot, grilled steak.

Each log of butter is sufficient for 10–12 steaks.

The roast beef you see to in advance; the salad you do just before you eat. Although, I should add, in case you're getting nervous, it doesn't spoil on sitting during the ordinary course of the evening (or indeed, lunch). And I love this salad either with the beef as it is or when hot; either way carved into tender pink slices and abundantly. I should also tell you that I make it often, in reduced form, as an easy but treaty supper for two, with a quickly grilled fillet steak, to be shared and sliced on top, tagliata-style, wafer thin and oozing its red juices over the tangy salad. This reduced form often means a lemon, peeled, sliced and chopped, left to steep in oil, salt, chilli and parsley while I'm cooking the steak and then tossed through a packet of designer leaves with some parmesan shaved off with a vegetable peeler. It follows, too, that the leaves indicated for the salad below are meant to be a suggestion only: I love the tough bitterness of radicchio alongside the juicy sourness of the lemons and toothsome saltiness of the shards of parmesan, but a plain green salad, boosted with the chilli-prinked lemon, is pretty damn fine as it is.

And whether you choose to eat the roast beef hot or cold with this, I implore you to add a pile of sweet, fluffy-tummied baked potatoes alongside. I wouldn't provide butter to melt within, though, but bowls of cold crème fraîche or soured cream flecked with chopped chives.

**2.5kg (or thereabouts) topside or contre fillet if you're feeling extravagant (or whatever cut of beef you prefer)**
**5 lemons**
**1 teaspoon Maldon salt**
**3 fresh red chillies, deseeded and finely chopped**

**5 tablespoons fresh parsley, chopped**
**5 tablespoons extra virgin olive oil**
**1 head frisée lettuce**
**2 heads radicchio**
**4 cos lettuce hearts**
**approx. 75g block parmesan**

Preheat the oven to 210°C/gas mark 7. For rare beef, cook for 12 minutes per 500g; it will continue cooking as it cools so be prepared to take it out of the oven when it still looks underdone to you. This should give you divinely ruby-rare roast beef; obviously, though, cook for longer if you want it less red. Anyway, set aside till cold. If, however, you're going to eat the roast beef rare and hot, then just stick it in the hottest oven you can for 15 minutes and then turn the oven down to 180°C/gas mark 4 and cook it for 15 minutes per 500g plus 15 minutes at the end. I'm hesitant about making this all sound too exact, because ovens vary enormously and the length of time it takes to roast rare roast beef in one oven can leave it either leathery and overcooked or still cold in the middle in another. Perhaps I exaggerate, but not by much. Probably the best advice is to say to go slowly and test often, though not by stabbing (you don't want to lose all those glorious red juices) but by pressing: when the beef's rare it will feel soft and eiderdown-bouncy to the touch; when medium rare it will feel springy; when well cooked it will have pretty much no bounce left in it. Of course, you can pierce with a knife to make really sure, but just try to leave that to the end, rather than puncture repeatedly throughout its cooking.

To make the salad, cut the tops and bottoms off the lemons. Sit them upright on a board on one end, and cut away the zest and pith from top to bottom with a sharp knife till only the juicy lemon remains. Now slice into rounds, then chop each round into about four, and place on a large plate or shallow bowl. Sprinkle the salt over them then scatter with the chopped chillies and parsley and pour over the oil. Leave to steep while you carve the beef and get on with the rest of the salad. Which simply means, tear the frisée, radicchio and cos lettuce hearts into rough pieces and mix together in a large bowl. Shave in most of the parmesan with a vegetable peeler and pour in most of the lemon chunks, and all of their oily juices. Mix together thoroughly with your fingers then decant into a couple of large, flat serving plates (I so much prefer salad on plates than in bowls), adding any more oil (or indeed lemon juice) if you think the dressing needs thus augmenting, then add the remaining lemon chunks and shave in a final few slithering curls of parmesan. I regard this as pretty well instant, all-year sunshine, so maybe here's the place to sneak in the suggestion that you consider this (perhaps with a squeeze of Seville orange juice should this be possible) with your leftover Christmas turkey. After all, when more do you need the hit of, even artificial, sun?

Serves 10.

POULTRY

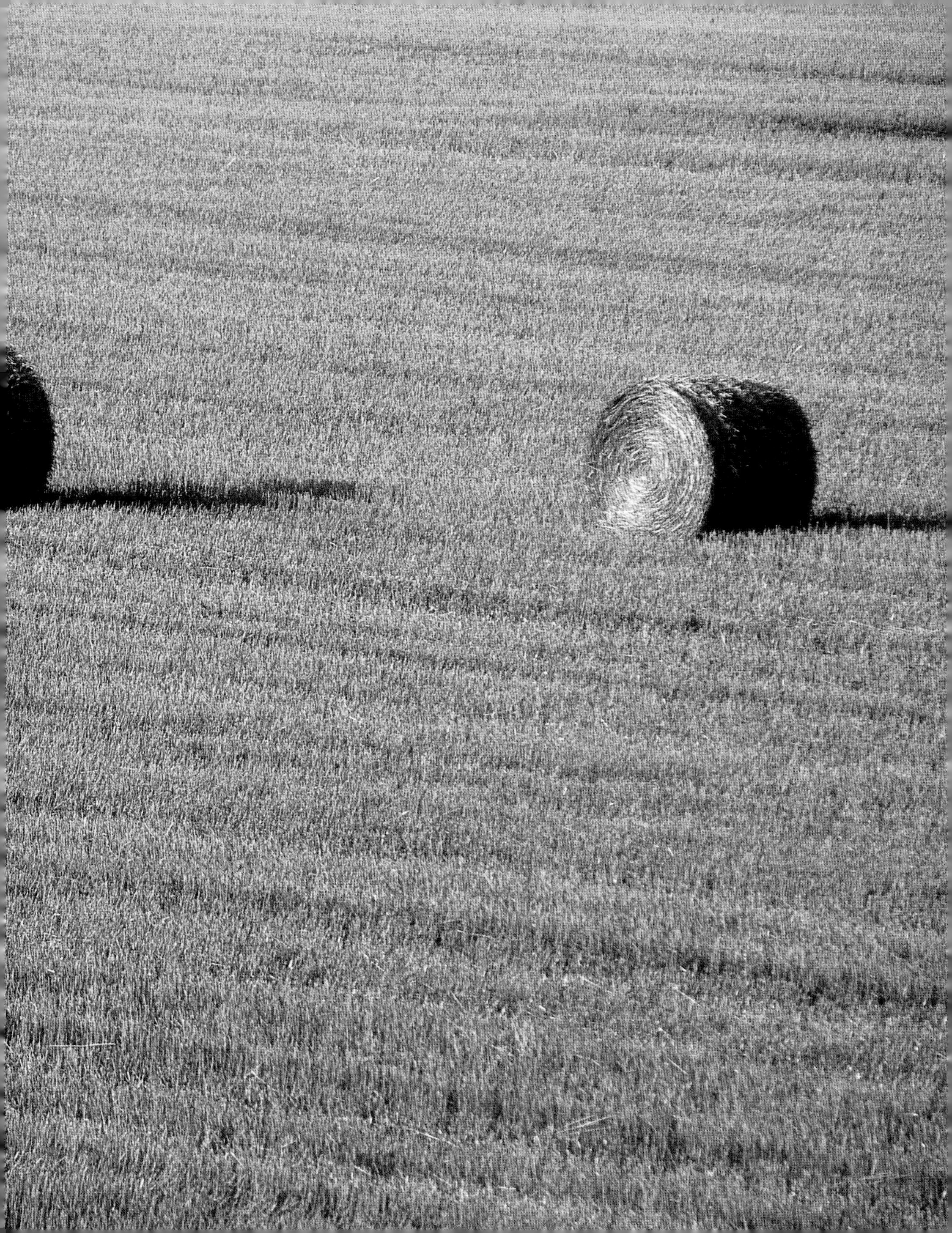

# FOUR CHICKEN SALADS

There is not much linking these salads save that they all start with the idea that you might have a piece of cold chicken leftover in the fridge. So even though each recipe seems to require one cold cooked chicken breast, it really doesn't matter which part of the chicken you're using or, unless it concerns you, how much. This sort of cooking – indeed my sort of cooking generally – isn't about weights and measures, but is just a matter of using what you've got how you want it.

## GOLDEN JUBILEE CHICKEN

This started off life as a reworking of Coronation Chicken, that mixture I can't help liking, against all contemporary culinary strictures, of cold chicken, mayo, mango chutney, curry powder and apricot purée (or that's how both my grandmothers made it). But still, I wanted to pare it down, make it lighter and fresher, and so this is it. Given the year of its inception, and its derivation, it seemed only historically right to rename it thus; believe me, no political affiliations are thereby intended.

1 mango, cut into approx. 1cm cubes

1 spring onion, finely chopped

1–2 red chillies (to taste), deseeded and finely chopped

juice of 1–2 limes (to taste)

1 cold cooked chicken breast, cut into chunks

1 Little Gem lettuce, sliced or shredded

1 large handful fresh coriander, chopped

1 teaspoon groundnut oil

few drops toasted sesame oil

Tumble the mango cubes, and any juice they make, into a bowl and, with your hands, mix in the chopped spring onion and chilli and squeeze over the lime juice: use as much or as little as you want; frankly, the amount of juice you can get from a lime varies enormously from one to another.

I tend to leave all these to steep while I get on with the rest of my shredding and chopping, but whatever way you do it, tumble in the chunked chicken and shredded lettuce and most of the coriander and, using your hands, toss to combine. Add the oils and toss again then decant on to a large serving plate and sprinkle over the remaining bit of coriander.

Serves 2–3.

# CAESAR CLEOPATRA

This is what I call – after a menu in the food court of an LA shopping mall – a Caesar salad with chicken in it. Best of all the chicken will have been grilled or griddled before being roughly shredded for the salad, but it's not obligatory. Since I seem to spend half my life teetering on the edge of a low-carbohydrate diet, I never put croutons in a Caesar salad (no hardship: I don't like them much anyway), but this is rather wonderful with the avocado. Yes, I know that once you've added chicken and avocado and dispensed with the croûtons and, as I also seem to have done, the anchovies, this is has absolutely no right at all calling itself any sort of Caesar salad, but you don't get to give a recipe a name like this that often, and I'm not passing it up now.

Of course, if you quite properly want to add anchovy, then just pound one soaked and drained salt-preserved little fish to a mush with the egg yolk when you start making the dressing – which again does not quite follow the normal procedures but does a very good job of its own; the chicken, after all, makes for a heavier salad, which requires in turn, a more creamily emulsified dressing.

2 cos lettuce hearts or 1 cos lettuce
1 egg yolk
2–3 tablespoons extra virgin olive oil
juice of half a smallish lemon
few drops Lea & Perrins

3 tablespoons freshly grated parmesan
1 cold, cooked chicken breast,
   preferably grilled
half an avocado (optional)

Tear the lettuce into large chunks and arrange on a plate. Mix up the dressing by whisking the egg yolk in a bowl and carry on whisking as you add the oil slowly. Whisk again adding the lemon juice and Lea & Perrins and pour over the lettuce, then toss well, preferably with your hands, so that all the leaves are coated. Sprinkle over 2 tablespoons of the parmesan and toss again. Cut the chicken into fat strips and add to the salad, along with the sliced avocado half, if you're using it. Toss again, then sprinkle over the final tablespoon of parmesan.

Serves 2.

# CHICKEN SALAD WITH SPINACH AND LARDONS

When I was a wee young thing, the spinach and lardons salad in Joe Allen's was considered quite the coolest thing – and I still love it, indeed love all those outdated, unfairly derided *salades tièdes* of yesteryear. These days I tend to use pancetta, which I cut myself into rugged little cubes, but can't quite help still calling these lardons here, out of deference to the whole ethos of this dish. Feel free, however to buy those ready-cubed, skinny pink lardons which come in cellophane packages at the supermarket – or indeed just snip up some streaky bacon and fry up these instead. I have no compunction whatsoever about using shop-bought packages of those tender bubby spinach leaves; for me, this would be a non-starter if I had to get the grit off *real* spinach myself.

1 teaspoon olive oil (not extra virgin)
200g lardons
1 x 200g packet young spinach leaves

1 cold, cooked chicken breast, sliced or shredded
1 tablespoon red wine vinegar

Put the teaspoon of oil in a heavy-bottomed frying pan over a medium to high heat and when it's warm add the lardons and fry till crispy, letting them ooze their salty juices into the pan; this will be the gloriously oily basis for the dressing later.

Toss the spinach leaves and chicken together in a bowl and when the lardons are cooked, take the pan off the heat and add them, too, transferring them with a slotted spatula, leaving the fat in the pan. Now stir the red wine vinegar into the pan, letting it hiss, bubble up and mix, and pour this on top of your salad. Quickly toss to mix: c'est ça.

Serves 1–2.

## CHICKEN, ALMOND AND PARSLEY SALAD

This came about the way most of my favourite food has come about, by greedy opportunism. I had some cold chicken in the fridge, a huge bunch of parsley in a jug by the stove and had recently opened a packet of flaked almonds and I was just too hungry to think further. The important thing is to leave the parsley whole and unchopped – just tear the leaves off the stalks and heap them on the plate in a rough jumble – and to toast the almonds, which just means tossing them about over medium heat in an oil-less pan until they take on colour, at the last minute. I want the heat from them as well as the crunch.

**1 cold cooked chicken breast, sliced and**
   **shredded**
**couple of handfuls fresh flat-leaf parsley**
**1 tablespoon or so extra virgin olive oil**

**juice of half a lemon**
**Maldon salt**
**50g or so flaked almonds, toasted**

Using your hands, mix the chicken and parsley together in a large bowl or on a large plate. Dribble over the olive oil and, still using your hands, toss to mix. Now squeeze over the lemon juice, sprinkle over the salt and tip in most of the toasted almonds and toss again. Sprinkle over the remaining almonds, and your work here on earth is done.
   Serves 1.

# ZA'ATAR CHICKEN WITH FATTOUSH

This is what I make just about every other time I have friends over in summer, and regularly during the rest of the year too for that matter. It's simple: the chicken deeply spiced with za'atar, that wonderful Middle-Eastern spice blend comprising thyme, sesame seeds and ground sumac, itself a glorious blood-red berry with an intensely astringent lemony tang; the salad a fresh tangle of mint, parsley, cucumber, tomato and spring onions, crumbled with torn shards of toasted pitta and sprinkled, again, with sumac. To be entirely proper, you should throw in some leafy, herbal purslane, too, but unless you happen to live near a Middle-Eastern shop, it's unlikely you'll be able to get your hands on any, so I haven't listed it below.

If you want to turn this into a real feast, then by all means supplement this oven-bronzed chicken in its nubbly, amber spices with the za'atar-marinated lamb kebabs on page 109. Know, too, that the za'atar itself is not the recondite ingredient it once would have been; my local supermarket stocks it, and the sumac, regularly, or you can order it from www.seasonedpioneers.co.uk, 0800 0682 348. I'm giving the recipe for the fattoush here simply because I've got in the habit of making these together, but this sour, refreshing Middle-Eastern bread salad has every right to an independent life of its own.

**for the chicken:**
**125ml olive oil (not extra virgin)**
**1 chicken (approx. 2–2.25kg), cut into 8 pieces**
**2 tablespoons za'atar**
**Maldon salt**

**for the fattoush:**
**2 pitta breads**
**3 fat spring onions, halved and sliced**

**1 cucumber, peeled, quartered lengthwise and chopped**
**3 tomatoes, diced**
**bunch fresh flat-leaf parsley, chopped**
**bunch fresh mint, chopped**
**1 clove garlic, minced**
**6–8 tablespoons extra virgin olive oil**
**juice of 1 lemon**
**Maldon salt**
**half a teaspoon sumac**

Pour the 125ml oil into a large roasting tin, big enough to fit all the chicken portions in a single layer, and then put in these very chicken portions, rubbing them about in the oil to give them a glossy coating. Sprinkle over the za'atar, and then work into the oily skin of the chicken so that each piece is well covered with the bosky, bark-coloured spices. Leave the meat to marinate for a couple of hours at room temperature. Or you can do all the marinating in my usual plastic-bag way (and see page 136 for example); which is certainly easier if you plan to marinate these much in advance – a day or two would be fine – and therefore need to stash them in the fridge.

Meanwhile, preheat the oven to 220°C/gas mark 8 and, when the chicken's had its aromatic steeping time, transfer the tin, making sure all the chicken pieces are skin side up, to the oven. If you've marinated the chicken in a freezer-bag, just tumble them out, pushing them skin side up, into a roasting tin, making absolutely sure you've squeezed over every last drop of the oily spice mixture they've been sitting in.

Roast the chicken portions for about 45 minutes, by which time they should be well cooked, which is how we want them here, and their spice-sprinkled skin burnished and crisp and baked to a fabulous burnt umber. Pile the pieces up, or arrange them as you like on a large flat plate and sprinkle over a little Maldon salt.

When the chicken's nearly cooked, you can get on with the fattoush. So, cut the pitta breads open lengthways so that you have four very thin halves, and lay them on a baking sheet. Toast them in the oven with the chicken for about 5 minutes to give them a bit of crunch then take them out and leave them somewhere to cool.

In a bowl, combine the spring onions, cucumber, tomatoes, parsley and mint and mince in the garlic. With a pair of kitchen scissors, cut the pitta into pieces over the bowl of salad – I tend to snip them into rough triangles – and drop them in, leaving a few back for the top. Toss the salad then dress it with the oil and lemon juice, tossing it again. Add some Maldon salt, and have a quick taste to see if the ratio of oil and lemon is right, adding more of either if necessary. Sprinkle over the reserved toasted pitta triangles and the lovely dark red, deeply bitter sumac, and serve the fattoush right alongside the za'atar chicken.

Serves 6.

I am almost embarrassed to tell you how often I eat this. So often in fact that I always have a couple of chickens, spatchcocked, in the marinade and vacuum-sealed (I'm a girl who can't resist a gadget) in plastic bags, waiting in the fridge, ready for the off at any given moment. The great thing about spatchcocked chicken – and forgive me if I've bored you with this before – is that it takes less time to cook than it does unflattened (so you're never more than three-quarters of an hour away from a proper dinner; another roasting tinful of diced new potatoes, mished around in a little olive or garlic-infused oil can cook away in the rack underneath at the same time) and you don't need to be good at carving. I just take a huge knife at it, and hack it into four greedy portions.

Obviously, you change the marinade as you wish. For one thing, I often leave out the onion altogether. And then, I sometimes steep the chicken just in a small amount of chopped tarragon, grated lemon zest and olive oil or go all-out fiery with smashed garlic, olive oil, a splosh of red wine vinegar and a small handful of crushed black peppercorns.

Any good butcher will spatchcock a chicken for you, or you could ask the butchery section at the supermarket to do it, but it's easy enough for you to manage yourself at home and I have to say I love a bit of DIY surgery. Just get a pair of poultry shears or tough scissors (I use a pair sold by someone on one of those door-to-door yellow duster trails, made for cutting through tins and tough stuff) and lay the chicken, breast side down, on a surface and cut through all along one side of the backbone. Then cut along the other side of the backbone and – hey presto – the backbone can be removed and you then turn the bird the other way up and press down as you open it out. You have in front of you a perfectly spatchcocked chicken, thirstily ready for its marinade. But if you're not up to this, life is not going to fall apart if you buy four chicken quarters instead.

1 spatchcocked chicken (approx. 2–2.25kg)
3 long sprigs fresh rosemary
juice of 1 lemon, plus more lemons to serve

1 red onion
100ml olive oil
Maldon salt

Put your spatchcocked chicken into a large freezer bag. Pull the waxily aromatic needles off 2 of the sprigs of rosemary and drop them on top. Now, cut the lemon in half and squeeze in the juice, chucking the empty shells in afterwards. Cut the onion into eighths (I can never be bothered to peel it) and add these to the bag, too. Pour in the olive oil and then tie up the bag and give it a good squidge around before sitting it in the fridge. And this is when, if you have the technology (and actually, as you might have guessed, my vacuum-sealer has been relegated to the cellar for some time now so, princess-like, I get my butcher to marinate and vacuum-pack my chickens for me) you can, instead of tying, vacuum-seal your bag and keep the chicken in the fridge like that for up to three weeks.

Marinate the chickens for a couple of hours out on the counter, or overnight – or for a couple of days – in the fridge.

To make a quick, brick-red Chilli Chicken, brush the skin of the spatchcocked bird with some sambal oelek, that hot and sharp chilli paste which you can find in every supermarket now, loosened up with a little vegetable oil.

When you're hungry, preheat the oven to 210°C/gas mark 7, and if you've marinated the chickens in the fridge, let them come to room temperature. Lay your flattened chicken, skin side up, on a tin lined with foil, along with the lemon husks and onion pieces, and add the remaining sprig of rosemary torn into a couple of pieces, tucking them between leg and breast. Cook for about 45 minutes by which time the chicken should be crisp skinned and tender within; you can even turn the oven down to about 150°C/gas mark 2 and let it remain in the oven long after it's cooked through. Somehow, this doesn't seem to make it stringily overcooked but, rather, infused with golden tenderness.

Take the tin out of the oven, cut the chicken into four pieces and arrange these on a plate, along with the onion bits, then pour over any syrupy golden juices from the tin and sprinkle generously with Maldon salt. Cut a lemon or two into quarters and scatter these clumpily about the chicken.

Serves 4 (and sometimes, I'm afraid, 2).

This is one of those recipes you just can't make once: that's to say, after the first time, you're hooked. It is gloriously easy: you just put everything in the roasting dish and leave it to cook in the oven, pervading the house, at any time of year, with the summer scent of lemon and thyme – and of course, mellow, almost honeyed garlic. I got the idea of it from those long-cooked French chicken casseroles with whole garlic cloves and just wanted to spritz it up with lemon for summer. The wonderful thing about it is that you turn the lemon from being a flavouring to being a major player; left in chunks to cook slowly in the oven they seem almost to caramelise and you can eat them, skin, pith and all, their sour bitterness sweetened in the heat.

**1 chicken (approx. 2–2.25kg), cut into 10 pieces**

**1 head garlic, separated into unpeeled cloves**

**2 unwaxed lemons, cut into chunky eighths**

**small handful fresh thyme**

**3 tablespoons olive oil**

**150ml white wine**

**black pepper**

Pre-heat the oven to 160°C/gas mark 3.

Put the chicken pieces into a roasting tin and add the garlic cloves, lemon chunks and the thyme; just roughly pull the leaves off the stalks, leaving some intact for strewing over later. Add the oil and using your hands mix everything together, then spread the mixture out, making sure all the chicken pieces are skin side up.

Sprinkle over the white wine and grind on some pepper, then cover tightly with foil and put in the oven to cook, at flavour-intensifyingly low heat, for 2 hours.

Remove the foil from the roasting tin, and turn up the oven to 200°C/gas mark 6. Cook the uncovered chicken for another 30–45 minutes, by which time the skin on the meat will have turned golden brown and the lemons will have begun to scorch and caramelise at the edges.

I like to serve this as it is, straight from the roasting tin: so just strew with your remaining thyme and dole out. This is wonderful, truly wonderful, with the braised Little Gem lettuces on page 155.

Serves 4–6.

# SICILIAN VINEGAR CHICKEN

This is a wonderfully sour, still mellow, chicken casserole which in winter I love to eat hot, as thin-sauced stew, out of a bowl, and in summer, left to cool to room temperature, its juices thickening on standing. It is also fabulous as a strange, soused salad: that's to say, absolutely cold, straight – even – from the fridge.

1 onion
100ml olive oil
1 chicken (approx. 2–2.25kg), skinned and jointed into 8 pieces
Maldon salt and black pepper
250ml chicken stock (fake is fine)
125ml dry white wine

125ml red wine vinegar
juice of half a lemon
handful fresh parsley, chopped, plus extra for sprinkling over at the end
small handful fresh basil leaves, chopped, plus extra for sprinkling over at the end
2 large tomatoes

Finely chop the onion and fry it gently, with some salt sprinkled over to stop it catching, in 4 tablespoons of the olive oil in a wide, heavy-bottomed pan for about 5 minutes, until it's softened but not browned.

Arrange the chicken pieces over the onion and season well with salt and pepper. Pour over the chicken stock, wine, vinegar and lemon juice, then sprinkle the parsley and basil over the top. Bring the pan to the boil and then cover and simmer gently for about 45 minutes.

Remove the lid and simmer away for about another 15 minutes, by which time the liquid should have reduced a little and the chicken itself be well cooked.

Blanch the tomatoes by putting them in a bowl and pouring over some boiling water from a kettle. Leave them there for 3 minutes or so then tumble them out, skin them, quarter them, remove the viscous glob of seeds and roughly chop the pink-red flesh. Mix them in a small bowl along with the remaining olive oil and some salt and pepper. I should admit here that I sometimes don't bother to blanch and peel the tomatoes, simply just deseed and chop them.

When the chicken is ready, remove the pieces to a large shallow bowl and, if you want the sauce any thicker, let it bubble away over a high heat to reduce further. If you've taken the blanched, peeled tomato route, then stir the tomato mixture into the sauce and pour it over the chicken waiting in its dish. If you've simply chopped the unpeeled tomatoes, then first pour the sauce over the chicken and then tumble the tomatoes around and, scantily, on top. Just before serving – which could be now or a whole lot later – sprinkle over a little more parsley and basil.

Serves 4.

# PICNIC-FRIED CHICKEN

I have to say, I am not a girl who goes in much for picnics, but I love picnic food. This is fried chicken as they make it in Italy: cut up small (you really have to bully your butcher on this one, or be a mean wielder of a cleaver yourself), marinated lemonly for edge and tenderness, then dipped into peppery flour, thence into beaten eggs and fried in olive oil. Actually, this is not quite as they make it in Italy: I introduce an Anglo note with the addition of English mustard powder (in the marinade as well as in the flour for dredging) to satisfy my need for heat. Cayenne would do the same job, of course, though use it more sparingly.

**1 chicken (approx. 2–2.25kg), cut into small pieces of about 5cm (I get about 22 x 50g pieces)**

**juice of 2 lemons**

**4 tablespoons olive oil**

**pinch of salt**

**good grinding of black pepper**

**2 cloves garlic, bruised**

**2 tablespoons English mustard powder**

**olive oil (not extra virgin) for frying**

*for the coating:*

**3 eggs**

**zest of 1 lemon**

**pinch of salt**

**125g plain, preferably Italian 00, flour**

**2 tablespoons English mustard powder**

Put the chicken pieces into a large shallow dish and marinate in the lemon juice, olive oil, salt and pepper, garlic and mustard powder for at least an hour, but if you cover the dish (or use the plastic-bag method) and put it in the fridge, you can leave it all marinating for up to a couple of days. Just make sure, when you want to fry it up, that it's really got to room temperature first.

When you're ready to get going, beat the eggs and lemon zest together in a large bowl and season with salt and pepper. Mix the flour and mustard powder together on a large flat plate, or easier still mix up half and just repeat once you've got through your first batch.

Pour in enough oil to come about 1cm up a large frying pan and heat till sizzling. Then dip the chicken pieces in the flour then the eggs, coating on all sides, and put carefully into the hot oil. Cook the meat until golden and crispy, about 15 minutes. You will have to be patient about this and proceed batch by small batch: don't crowd the pan or the temperature of the oil will drop too much and the chicken will be greasy rather than crisp and crunchy.

I love this warm rather than hot – and cold's good too – eaten with my fingers and dipped into some more English mustard (though made up, rather than powder this time) as I go. Spritzed with lemon and sprinkled with Maldon salt is also fabulous.

Serves 6–8.

# SAFFRON-SCENTED CHICKEN PILAF

Call me Scheherazade, but I'm in my turquoise gauze veil and jewelled slippers for this one. The cinnamon and lemony yoghurt marinade gives the chicken a soft, perfumed tenderness; the saffron in the rice, itself studded with nuts and the musky breath of cardamom, is almost lit up with gold. Cook this and people will want gratefully to strew your path with rose petals for evermore.

**500g chicken breast, cut into 2 x 1cm pieces (please don't get your ruler out: I mean this as an approx. guide only)**
**1 x 200g tub Greek yoghurt**
**juice of half a lemon**
**quarter teaspoon ground cinnamon**
**half a teaspoon saffron threads**
**1 litre chicken stock (instant bouillon concentrate is, as ever, fine)**
**15g unsalted butter**

**2–3 tablespoons groundnut oil**
**500g basmati rice**
**3–4 cardamom pods, bruised**
**juice and zest of 1 lemon**
**50g cashew nuts**
**50g flaked almonds**
**25g pine nuts**
**3–4 tablespoons shelled pistachio nuts**
**small bunch fresh parsley, chopped**

Marinate the chicken pieces in the yoghurt, lemon and cinnamon for about an hour. Soak the saffron threads in the chicken stock.

Over medium heat, in a large pan with a lid, melt the butter along with 1 tablespoon oil and add the rice, stirring it to coat until glossy. Pour in the saffron and chicken stock, add the cardamom pods, lemon juice and zest and bring the pan to the boil, then clamp on a lid and turn the heat down to very low; a heat diffuser, if you've got one, would be good here. Cook like this for about 10–15 minutes, by which time the rice should have absorbed the liquid and be cooked through.

While the rice is cooking, shake the excess yoghurt marinade off the chicken using a sieve. Then fry the meat in a hot pan with the remaining spoonful or so of oil, and do this in batches so that the chicken colours rather than just pallidly stews to cookedness.

When the rice is cooked, take it off the heat and fork through the pan-bronzed chicken pieces. Toast all the nuts except the pistachios, by simply shaking them in an oil-less frying-pan over a medium heat until they colour and begin to give off their waxy scent, and then add them to the pilaf along with the chopped parsley. Pile everything on to a plate and add a fabulously green sprinkling of slivered or roughly chopped pistachios.

Serves 6.

# CHICKEN AND CASHEW NUT CURRY

This is the softest, most mellow of curries, by which I don't mean so much that it's mild but that it has a gently lapping warmth rather than fierce bite. I always need to keep the chilli content relatively high – I can't see the point in an entirely toothless Ruby Murray – but the Southern Indian notes of cardamom and coconut milk, and the waxy fatness of the cashews, the soured cream added at the end, keep it calm and voluptuously resonant. I like this with a bowlful of basmati rice, cooked plain save for some bruised cardamom pods added along with the water.

3 tablespoons groundnut oil
2 small onions, finely chopped
salt
2cm fresh ginger, minced
1 fat clove garlic, minced
2 small green chillies, deseeded and
  finely chopped
1 teaspoon turmeric
1 teaspoon ground cumin
1 teaspoon ground coriander
1 x 400ml tin coconut milk

250ml strongly flavoured chicken stock
  (I use bouillon concentrate made up
  with water)
4 cardamom pods, bruised
1kg boned, skinned chicken thighs, cut
  into bite-sized pieces
200g fine beans, topped, tailed and
  halved
125g cashew nuts
3 tablespoons soured cream
small bunch fresh coriander, chopped

Heat the oil in a wide saucepan and fry the onions gently, sprinkled with a little salt to stop them burning, until softened and then add the ginger, garlic, chillies, turmeric, cumin and coriander and cook, stirring, for another minute or so.

Stir the coconut milk and stock into the onion spice paste and when everything is incorporated add the cardamom and chicken pieces. Bring the curry back to the boil and then turn down the heat and simmer gently for about 10 minutes or until the chicken is just about cooked through. Check the seasoning and add the fine beans, cooking for another 5 minutes or so. While you're waiting for them to cook, toast the cashew nuts in a dry frying pan until coloured a little, then tip in the cashew nuts and stir in the soured cream and half of the chopped coriander. Ladle into bowls, sprinkling with more of the coriander as you go.

Serves 6.

You can sneer all you like about duck à l'orange but that bird, this fruit: they do go together. And I love the combination this way: the *magrets* steeped in ginger and orange and quickly fried or grilled and just sliced thinly, while still pink within, to ooze their robust juices over some finely sliced red onions and salt-sprinkled oranges. An old idea, maybe, but so fresh – and a whole lot easier than the méthode originale.

**2 duck breasts**

**for the marinade:**
**juice and zest of 1 orange**
**1cm fresh ginger, minced**
**1 small red onion, roughly chopped**

**for the salad:**
**2 red onions**
**4 navel oranges**
**Maldon salt**
**small bunch fresh parsley finely chopped**
  **(or coriander)**

Slash the fat on the duck breasts in diagonals, then put them in the mixed marinade ingredients for about an hour.

Peel, halve and slice the red onions for the salad into very thin half-moons and put them in a bowl. Cut off the top and bottom of the oranges, then, using a small knife, cut vertically around each one to remove the skin and pith. Halve each orange, cut into slices and tip, with all the juice they make as you slice them, into the bowl with the onion.

Leave this orange and onion mixture to steep while you fry the duck. Heat a dry frying pan and put the meat in skin side down. Cook for about 15 minutes in total, turning the duck periodically so that both sides are well coloured; obviously small duck breasts will need less time.

Leave the duck to rest while you arrange the salad on a large flat plate and give a good sprinkle with Maldon salt. Slice the meat thinly on the diagonal and lay the slices on top of the orange and onion. Pour over any orangey, gingery, bloody juices and sprinkle robustly with parsley – or, if you prefer, coriander.

Serves 4.

# BARBECUED QUAIL

I love these sweet and meaty quail, conker-shiny in their vaguely Chinesey marinade. As often as not, I grill them rather than barbecue them; even a blitz in a very hot oven will do. The thing is to marinate them for a good long time – at least 24 hours – so that they keep fleshy and juicy and meltingly tender no matter how brutally you cook them.

**10 quail**

*For the marinade:*
**125ml soy sauce**
**6 tablespoons roasted sesame oil**

**1 x 250g jar hoisin sauce**
**3 tablespoons rice vinegar**
**5cm knob fresh ginger, minced**
**2 cloves garlic, minced**
**juice of 1 orange**

You need the quail to be spatchcocked which is, given their poor little frail bones, a very easy job. First trim their wing tips with a pair of kitchen shears or, frankly, scissors, then cut along both sides of the backbone, remove it, and squish each quail down flat.

Mix all the ingredients for the marinade in a large measuring jug, whisk to mix, then divide the mixture between two large freezer bags. Chuck in the flattened quail, half in each, then tie up the bags; or you can simply lay the quail in a couple of dishes, pour the marinade over and cover with clingfilm. Leave in the fridge for at least 24 hours; 48 wouldn't hurt.

Make sure you take them out of the fridge in enough time to get to room temperature before you cook them. They shouldn't need more than 10 minutes on a hot barbecue, under a hot grill or in a very hot oven.

Serves 4–5.

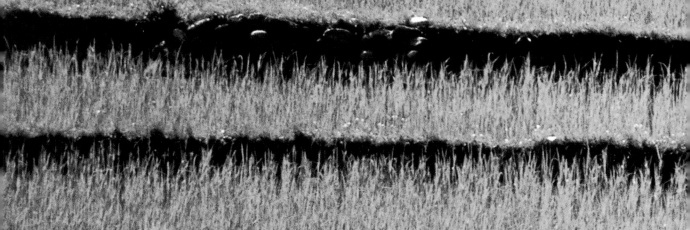

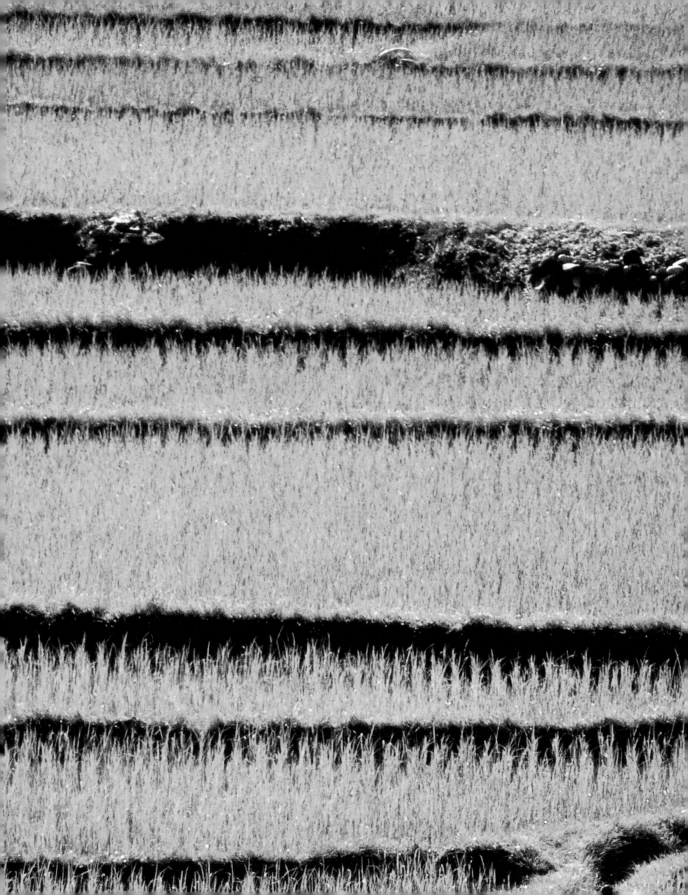

# HASSELBACK POTATOES

I think of these Swedish roast potatoes as being rather like sautéed potatoes on the stem: each one is cut into thin slices across almost right through, but not quite, and then roasted in buttery oil; as they cook, the potatoes fan out, like slightly fleshy crisps with their bottoms still attached. Traditionally, maincrop potatoes are used, but I love these made with new potatoes, too; in which case, Charlotte or Ratte, which are waxy-fleshed and taperingly oval in shape, are best. If you're using maincrop potatoes, avoid those huge floury monsters; moderately proportioned Cara potatoes, or similar, would be just fine for the job.

The advantage of using new potatoes is that they take less time to cook, but the disadvantage is that they take longer to prepare. Finely slicing a lot of little potatoes is a much more fiddly exercise. But whatever size of potato you're using, the important thing is not to cut the whole way through. I find the easist way of doing this is by putting the potato in the bowl of a wooden spoon while I slice it; the outer edges of the spoon – if you understand what I mean – prevent your being able to get your knife right through to the bottom of the potato which is cradled in it, so you couldn't botch the job even if you wanted to. The potato has to fit in the spoon for this to work, so use a larger one for maincrop potatoes, a small one for new potatoes. It's as simple as that.

If you want to peel the potatoes, do, but I find it isn't necessary. And if I buy those shiny, pebbly supermarket ones, I don't even scrub them.

| | |
|---|---|
| **18 medium oval-shaped potatoes, about 125g each, or 36 new potatoes, approx. 60g each** | **45g butter** |
| | **5 tablespoons olive oil** |
| | **Maldon salt** |

If you're using the larger potatoes, preheat the oven to 210°C/gas mark 7; for roasting new potatoes, preheat to 200°C/gas mark 6. Put each potato, in turn, in the bowl of a wooden spoon, like you would carry an egg in an egg-and-spoon race, and cut across at about 3mm intervals. When you've cut them all, put the baking tin on the hob with the butter and oil and heat up till sizzling. Turn the potatoes well, putting them in upside down (ie, cut side down) first, then the right side up, and spoon the fat over them. Sprinkle each potato well with salt and put in the oven: cook the large potatoes for about an hour and 10 minutes, testing to see whether the flesh is soft (you may need another 10 minutes for this); 40 minutes should be fine for the new potatoes. Transfer to a warmed plate, and serve. When I'm truly warming to my Swedish theme, I serve these with the seared mustard-coated salmon on page 97 and raw beetroot salad on page 54, but at other times I'm happy to make them to go with almost anything.

Serves 6.

# CAPONATA

Think Sicilian ratatouille or thereabouts, in which the tastes of all the vegetables keep their distinctness rather than merging into a soupy stew. This is Anna del Conte's version (only I am more slovenly and don't soak the aubergines as she requests) from her revised and expanded *Gastronomy of Italy* which is the book I always turn to when I want to see how something is really done *all'Italiana*.

I love this by itself, with lemony roast chicken, alongside plain grilled white fish, hunks of pink-grilled lamb or just to pick at from the fridge.

**2 medium aubergines**
**3–5 tablespoons vegetable oil for frying**
**Maldon salt and black pepper**
**1 head celery**
**3 tablespoons olive oil**
**1 large onion, finely chopped**
**1 x 225g tin plum tomatoes, drained and chopped**

**1 tablespoon caster sugar**
**6 tablespoons white wine vinegar**
**1 tablespoon grated dark chocolate**
**4 tablespoons salted capers, soaked and rinsed**
**50g pitted green olives**
**1 hard-boiled egg**

Cut the aubergines into 1cm cubes and fry them in the vegetable oil (using as much as you need) in two batches until golden brown. Remove them to a plate and sprinkle with Maldon salt.

Remove the tougher outer stalks of the celery, then cut the inner stalks into similar sized pieces as the aubergine and fry them in the same way. Then put them on the plate with the aubergine.

Pour the olive oil into the frying pan and add the chopped onion, frying it gently until soft but not coloured. Now tumble in the tomatoes and cook them along with the onions for about 10 minutes, seasoning with salt and pepper.

In a separate saucepan heat the sugar and vinegar, and then add the chocolate, capers and olives, simmering gently to melt the chocolate. You may think the chocolate an outlandish addition: it isn't. It must be dark chocolate, though, to give depth and rounded bitterness. Add this highly-flavoured mixture to the tomato sauce and cook for a further 5 minutes.

Now, stir in the aubergine and celery, and cook everything together, to let the flavours develop, for about 10–15 minutes.

Arrange the caponata on a large flat plate or a bowl (as you like) and push the boiled egg through a small sieve to decorate the top. You can leave this out if you want: the taste will not be impaired. But there's something so sunnily retro about that mimosa-garnish of hard-boiled egg. The shinily dark colours of the caponata are suddenly lifted, made alive. An eggless version will need, instead, a similarly refreshing sprinkle of parsley.

Serves 4–6.

I know you may think you've done roast vegetables to death, but these are different: small, intensely flavoured new season's potatoes, carrots, courgettes, garlic somehow turned buttery by the oven's intense heat.

You could braise them all with some oil, butter, bouillon or water in a large shallow pan – and the French often do – but I suggest the oven not only because it seems to point up the vegetables' sweetness and fresh flavour, but also because as far as I'm concerned any cooking that involves stashing food in the oven, takes away some of that feeling of slaving under pressure.

If you can't get fresh garlic – those as yet uncloved, aromatically damp bulbs – then use a head of ordinary garlic and just separate the cloves, leaving them unpeeled, and scatter them among the other vegetables.

**500g small new potatoes, halved**
**salt**
**4 baby marrows, halved and quartered**
**3 small turnips, peeled, halved and**
  **quartered**
**2 heads fresh garlic, halved and**
  **quartered**

**2 bunches baby carrots, trimmed**
  **of their leaves**
**100g baby leeks, trimmed and left whole**
**4 tablespoons olive oil (not extra virgin)**
  **or more as needed for roasting the**
  **vegetables**

Bring a largeish pan of water to the boil, and when it starts boiling add salt and then the potatoes, and let them boil for 10 minutes. Preheat the oven to 200°C/gas mark 6.

Drain the potatoes well, and put them into a large roasting dish with all the other vegetables. Give everything a good coating of olive oil, and roast for about 35–45 minutes, by which time all the vegetables should be cooked, tender within and crisped and coloured, in parts, on top.

Serves 6.

If you thought that lettuce had texture rather than flavour – an easy assumption if most of your salad is supermarketed and plastic-wrapped – then try cooking it. The tightly budded leaves become tender and, infused with chicken stock (for which the usual pro-visos hold), take on a delicate herbalness. I love these soft jade bundles with the slow-roasted garlic and lemon chicken on page 138, but try them too with a plain, lemony roast chicken. Any pan juices left make a wonderfully, soothing, single portion of light summer broth.

**6 Little Gem lettuces, left whole**
**500ml chicken stock**
**60ml extra virgin olive oil**

**handful fresh thyme sprigs**
**salt and black pepper**

Pre-heat the oven to 200°C/gas mark 6.

Cut the ends off the lettuce, and remove any discoloured outer leaves. Lay the Little Gems snugly in a baking dish, then pour in the chicken stock. Drizzle over the oil and pull the leaves off the sprigs of thyme and sprinkle them over, then season with salt and pepper.

Cover the dish tightly with foil, and put it in the preheated oven for about 20 minutes or until the lettuces are softly wilting and tender.

Serves 6.

# COURGETTE FRITTERS

I know the word fritter conjures up a complex world of deep-frying and dense-eating, but these are light, simple babies – just grated courgettes, mixed with feta, herbs and spring onions, stirred up with flour and eggs and dolloped into a frying pan to make little vegetable pancakes which, unlike most fried food, are best eaten not straight out of the pan, but left to cool to room temperature. This takes any slaving over a hot stove element out of the equation: you just spoon serenely away over your pan before anyone's around.

I like these best as a starter – or just as they are, along with a green salad, for a meat-free, summer's lunch.

| | |
|---|---|
| **4 courgettes (approx. 750g)** | **1 teaspoon paprika** |
| **5–6 spring onions, finely chopped** | **140g plain flour** |
| **250g feta cheese** | **salt and pepper** |
| **small bunch fresh parsley, chopped** | **3 eggs, beaten** |
| **small bunch fresh mint, chopped, plus** | **olive oil for frying** |
| **extra to sprinkle over at the end** | **3–4 limes** |
| **1 tablespoon dried mint** | |

Coarsely grate the courgettes with either the grating blade in the processor or by hand. Spread the little shards out on a tea towel and leave for about 20 minutes to get rid of any excess wetness.

Put the chopped spring onions in a bowl and crumble in the feta. Stir in the chopped parsley and mint, along with the dried mint and paprika. Add the flour and season well with salt and pepper. Gradually add the beaten egg and mix thoroughly before stirring in the drained, grated courgettes. Don't be alarmed by the unflowing straggly lumpiness of this batter; it's meant to be this way.

Heat a few tablespoons of oil in a large frying pan and drop heaped dessertspoons of the mixture into the hot oil, flattening the little cakes down with the back of the spoon as you go. Cook these little patties for about 2 minutes each side until golden, and then transfer to a couple of waiting plates.

Chop up the limes and tumble them about the edges of the plates. Sprinkle over a little more chopped mint and eat them just as they are, spritzed with lime juice as you go.

Makes about 25.

# GREEN VEGETABLE CURRY

Look, I know green curry is hardly hot culinary news, but I don't think it's possible to be reminded too often how wonderful it is. This is a meat-free version, to serve either to vegetarians, just with rice or noodles, or as an aromatic side dish to go with something that has enough body to stand up to it but a gentle enough flavour not to fight with it: grilled monkfish or unsauced, lime-sharpened chicken breasts would be just right.

1 x 400ml tin of coconut milk

1 tablespoon green Thai curry paste

1 lemongrass stalk, bruised and cut in half lengthwise

2 lime leaves, roughly shredded

1–2 tablespoons Thai fish sauce

2–3cm fresh ginger, peeled and chopped

1 teaspoon caster sugar

300ml vegetable stock

75g baby corn, cut into thirds at an angle

250g asparagus, chopped at an angle into 3cm pieces

200g pak choi, sliced so that stalks and greens are separate

200g fine beans, topped and tailed

125g sugar snaps

juice of 1 lime

3 tablespoons chopped fresh coriander

In a large wide pan, over medium heat, whisk a little of the coconut milk into the Thai paste. Let it bubble away for a couple of minutes, then stir in the rest of the coconut milk. Put the lemongrass, lime leaves, fish sauce, ginger, sugar and stock into the pan and bring to the boil. Add the baby corn first, and let these cook for 5 minutes, then add the asparagus and after a couple of minutes, the pak choi stalks and fine beans. Let the pan come back up to the boil, and after a minute add the sugar snaps and pak choi greens. These won't need more than a minute: everything should look vibrantly green and still taste a bit squeaky. Take off the heat and add the lime juice and check the seasoning. Sprinkle with the coriander before serving.

    Serves 4.

# MOUTABAL

I have recently emerged from a complicated and long-standing love-hate relationship with aubergines generally, but for this smoky, buff-coloured, sesame-thick and lemon-sharp purée I have always had an unqualified, unreserved passion. It also happens to work wonderfully with roast, barbecued or griddled lamb, as a kind of thick dipping sauce. But don't think of it exclusively in that light: eat it squashed into pitta, or dunk thick batons of raw vegetables in it; or serve it alongside bowls of hummus (the bought kind if you want, fiddled about with as on page 120) and tabbouleh (a version of which appears on page 111).

I find it easiest to make it in advance bar the garlic, then just mince or crush and stir the garlic in at the last moment. But whatever, this is a very simple procedure. A griddle (or barbecue) is best for cooking the aubergines, since by charring them you infuse the flesh with the requisite smokiness, but to be honest (just because it's the least hassle) I mostly cook them in the oven.

Try and buy the tahina – that clay-like sesame paste – from a Middle-Eastern shop if you can, otherwise you can resort to any healthstore.

**3 aubergines**
**4 tablespoons tahina**
**Maldon salt**
**juice of one to one and a half lemons**

**3 cloves garlic**
**1 tablespoon or so extra virgin olive oil**
**1 pomegranate (optional) or small bunch fresh flat-leaf parsley, chopped**

If you're going to griddle the aubergines, then prick them a few times with the tines of a fork and then cook them for about 20 minutes a side on a hot griddle (or under a hot grill) until they've deflated and shrivelled and are pulpily soft in the middle, charred on the outside. If you're baking them, put them, pricked as above, in a 210°C/gas mark 7 oven for about an hour, till the skin's blackened and the flesh soft. In either case, remove when cooked and set aside till cool enough to handle. Put a large sieve over a bowl and then cut open the aubergines and spoon the soft pulp into the sieve. Leave to drain for about a quarter of an hour.

In a large bowl, using a fork, mix the tahina with a tablespoonful of warm water and a teaspoon of Maldon salt, then stir the lemon juice into the mixture. Turn the dry aubergine pulp into this, and mash with a fork till all's combined. When you want to eat it, add the garlic, chopped very fine or crushed, then turn into a shallowish bowl, drizzle with a little olive oil and, if you feel so authentically inclined, dot with a few scarlet glassy beads of pomegranate. I admit it's hard, if not impossible to get pomegranates over here in summer, but don't panic: just sprinkle over some freshly chopped flat-leaf parsley instead. The flavours of this moodily buff-coloured purée are fabulous enough; it's last minute, vivifying colour it needs.

Serves about 8 as part of a mezze.

For all that you need to clatter about with Springform tins and baking sheets, this is remarkably easy to make. I always seem to have spare egg white knocking around, which also inclines me to cook it. But it's worth making the – slight – effort even if you have to put aside the yolks for use elsewhere. This makes a wonderful summer starter or light lunch, the latter either by itself or rustled up as a vegetarian-pleaser.

If you want to forgo the grilled radicchio alongside, then do and just make a green salad to go with it, but the combination, as it stands, is perfect: the heat-wilted radicchio loses some of its bitterness, but keeps just enough perfectly to offset the delicate, not-quite-blandness of the ricotta. The summer-scentedness of thyme deliciously permeates both.

**for the baked ricotta:**
**500g ricotta cheese**
**2 egg whites, lightly beaten**
**1 tablespoon chopped fresh thyme**
**zest of 1 lemon**
**salt and pepper**
**2 tablespoons olive oil**

**for the radicchio:**
**approx. 6 tablespoons olive oil**
**2 tablespoons chopped fresh thyme**
**1 large radicchio, cut into eighths**
  **lengthways**
**1 lemon to serve**

Pre-heat the oven to 180°C/gas mark 4.

Mix the ricotta with the beaten egg whites and add most of the chopped thyme, the lemon zest and salt and pepper.

Brush a 20cm Springform tin with oil, and pour in the ricotta mixture then drizzle with olive oil and scatter a little more chopped thyme over the top. Don't be alarmed at how shallow this is; it is not intended to be other than a slim disc.

Place on a baking sheet and cook in the oven for about 30 minutes. The baked ricotta will rise a little and set dry on top, but will not turn a golden colour like a cake.

Let the tin cool a little before springing open, and removing to a plate. Leave to cool a little longer, then cut into wedges and eat, still warm, with the radicchio.

Talking of which, you should get on with this just before serving, which really means preheating the grill while the ricotta-cake is cooling. Mix the olive oil and thyme in a shallow bowl, and then wipe the radicchio slices in the herby oil before grilling them for a few minutes, turning them as necessary, until slightly wilted and golden at the edges.

Add a squeeze of lemon at the end before serving with the baked ricotta.

Serves 4–6.

# CORSICAN OMELETTE

Bear with me – as telephonists like to say – while I gush for a bit. This has to be the world's best omelette. I call it Corsican not because it stems from any in-depth research into, or indeed intimate knowledge of, the food of Corsica but because it is the adaptation, from memory, of the best thing I ate there on a holiday now nearly 17 years ago. Also, to be fair, the key ingredient is itself Corsican, *brocciu*, a soft goat's whey cheese that's left to drain and shape in woven baskets; think ricotta with an edge. You sometimes come across this omelette in a sweetened version, with sugar sprinkled along with the mint (a herb that the Corsicans use much more in their cooking than the French) but I like it sharp and savoury. I'm not pretending that you can get brocciu here, but that hasn't ever stopped me making it: I just use that goat's cheese – chèvre – that comes in a log and which is incredibly easy to come by. Cut away the soft-kid skin and crumble the white sharp cheese into the eggs in the pan: the salty sharpness contrasts exquisitely with the rich fattiness of the eggs; against which, too, the fresh hit of mint is positively exhilarating, though to tell the truth, I make this just as often (just because it's easier to keep both chèvre and eggs in the fridge on constant standby) without it.

Think of this more as a lunch or supper dish, although I wouldn't turn it down at any time of day.

| | |
|---|---|
| **3 eggs** | **leaves from 3–4 good-sized sprigs fresh** |
| **salt and pepper** | **mint, shredded** |
| **15g butter** | **approx. 100g thick slice of a chèvre log** |

Beat the eggs and season with salt and pepper. Melt the butter in a frying pan approximately 25cm in diameter.

When the butter has melted and is bubbling, throw in most of the shredded mint, saving some for sprinkling on top at the end. When it has sizzled in the butter and become vibrantly green, pour in the beaten eggs and tip the egg around the pan. Crumble the cheese over the omelette and cook, lifting the sides and swilling the pan around to let any runny egg cook in the heat underneath.

When the top of the omelette looks nearly set but still gooey, fold into three lengthways – in other words, fold in two sides, leaving a strip of white-blobbed omelette facing up in a strip in the middle – and slide on to a plate. Sprinkle with the reserved mint and eat.

Serves 1.

# POTATO AND PEA FRITTATA

A frittata is an Italian omelette: thick, unfolded and cooked on one side in a pan on the hob, then, to make sure the whole's cooked through, placed still in its pan under the grill for a few minutes. At least I find this the easiest way: I am not sanguine about flipping the thing over unless I make mini ones (as I often do) in my blini pan. But actually, none of this is hard. And you may find it difficult to believe me, but it actually tastes at its best cold. Not fridge cold, just completely cool. Of course you can use anything to go in: I just love the sweet meatiness of the oniony peas and potatoes. And of course, in this respect, fresh peas would be best, or at least more authentically summery, but I'd be a vile and lying monster if I didn't confess that I make this myself with frozen . . .

**100g new potatoes, diced**
**75g frozen peas, thawed, or 150g fresh**
  **peas, podded**
**3 tablespoons olive oil**

**1 medium onion, finely diced**
**8 large eggs**
**salt and pepper**
**4 tablespoons freshly grated parmesan**

Bring the diced potatoes to the boil in salted water and boil briskly for 5 minutes, then drain. Put the peas into a bowl, pour over some boiling water from the kettle and leave them until you're ready to add them to the frittata, later. If you have more energy than me and are using fresh peas, then cook them along with the potatoes.

Turn on the grill – you want it to be good and hot later – and heat the oil in a heavy-based or non-stick frying pan of about 25cm diameter, and fry the onion until it begins to soften, then add the potatoes and cook for about 10 minutes or until the mixture's cooked, but don't let it burn or turn too brown. You want to emphasise its sweet softness, with nothing crisp about it.

Add the drained peas for the last couple of minutes of cooking, then transfer this mixture to a large bowl and let cool slightly.

Break the eggs into the bowl, and beat to mix. Season with salt and pepper and add the parmesan.

Put your frying pan back on to the heat; it should still be nice and oily. Then pour the egg mixture into the frying pan and cook over a medium heat for about 8 minutes, or until the frittata is set more or less, save for a still-gooey top.

When you think you've got to this stage – remembering that the frittata will continue cooking as it cools, and moreover you want an element of oozy interior – take the pan off the hob and put it under the grill until the top's golden and just set and beginning to puff up slightly. Ease around the edges of the pan with a knife or spatula to loosen the frittata but don't dig at it too much or the frittata will not keep its crisp borders and smooth shape. Place a large flat plate on top of the pan, then up-end them both, so the plate's underneath and the pan's on top. Remove pan and – hey presto – you've got a beautiful, golden flecked omelette staring up at you. Leave to cool (or eat warm if you prefer). Cut into wedges to serve.

Makes about 6 wedges.

# GARLIC BREAD

You won't find me turning my nose up at even the most unreconstructed, baguette-bound garlic bread, but I happen to be particularly besotted with this version, made cross-culturally, with small, puffy-tummied, spindle-tipped Indian breads to form almost gondola-shaped individual loaves for greedy people.

The stipulation of unsalted butter followed by the addition of salt is not as mad as it seems: unsalted butter just has a better taste; and nothing gives a more desirable saltiness than Maldon (and no, I am not on the payroll).

**175g unsalted butter**
**4 cloves garlic, minced, preferably by**
**microplane**

**sprinkling of Maldon salt**
**2 Barbari nans**

Mix the butter and garlic with some salt – you can do this in the processor if that helps – and slash the Barbari nans at angles; about 4 cuts per little loaf should be about right. Spread the butter generously into the cuts you have made, then wrap the nans in foil and put them on a baking sheet.

When you are ready – and you can sit them thus prepared for hours if you want – pre-heat the oven to 200°C/gas mark 6, and cook the foil-wrapped breads for about 15 minutes, then open the foil loosely and let the breads crisp up a bit on the top for about 5 minutes before you take them out of the oven.

Give each person their own, semi-unwrapped loaf, still in its foil. Children, who seem to love both garlic bread and individually portioned food (sharing not being a strong point with them) tend to be mad about these – or mine are (at time of going to press at least).

Serves 2.

# PUDDINGS

# RICOTTA HOTCAKES

These are breakfast pancakes summer-style, ridiculously light, and lemony somehow even without the addition (for a change in this book) of lemon. If you imagine the flavour of cheesecake combined with a texture that's best, if wordily, described as a kind of souffléed griddle cake, you're somewhere near getting the measure of these. My tip, however, is to cut to the chase and make them yourself. Serve, outside if weather and property ownership permits, with some chopped ripe strawberries, partially crushed with a fork, tumbling on top. There is a vocal syrup-dousing contingent in my house, but in my view it mars their fabulous delicacy and, besides, the accompanying fruit allows you to delude yourself that these are healthy.

250g ricotta cheese

125ml semi-skimmed milk

2 large eggs, separated

100g plain flour

1 teaspoon baking powder

pinch salt

2 teaspoons groundnut oil

*to serve:*

250g strawberries, chopped (or other
   berries of your choice, of course)

Put the ricotta, milk and egg yolks into a bowl and mix well to combine. Stir in the flour, baking powder and salt and gently whisk to make a smooth batter.

Beat the egg whites until they become foamy – this isn't hard work even, whisking by hand, which is all that's needed here – and then fold them into the ricotta mixture.

Heat the oil in a large frying pan and drop in heaped dessertspoons of batter. Cook the pancakes for about 1 minute until golden and then flip them over and cook for another minute. Keep the cooked pancakes warm, by tenting with foil on a large warmed plate, while you work your way through the batter, and then serve with syrup – if you must – and strawberries.

Makes about 25.

# CARAMELISED PINEAPPLE WITH HOT CHOCOLATE SAUCE

There's no other way to put this: these are fruit kebabs. I know how this sounds, but that's not how they taste.

Now that we've got that over with, I'll go on: these skewer-threaded chunks of pineapple are sprinkled with sugar and blitzed on the barbecue or under the grill till that absurdly yellow, tropical-sunshine flesh is scorched a deep, golden brown. Just when you thought it couldn't get any better, there is more. You make a thick, dark coconut-rum-deepened chocolate sauce and dip the pineapple into it as you eat. For hygiene's sake, and it's not often you'll hear me saying that, it might be wise to give each person their own little bowl of molten, Malibued chocolate sauce for repeated, fondue-style dunkings, though you can simply stick a ladle in a big bowl of the stuff and let everyone spoon the sauce over the pineapple, on their plates, as they eat. To make this less a Barbie-fest, however, you can forget the bamboo skewer element and simply sugar and grill pieces of pineapple and serve them up to be eaten relatively elegantly, with knife and fork, a jugful of hot chocolate sauce on the table alongside.

**1 ripe pineapple**
**approx. 250g demerara sugar**

**125ml Malibu**
**120ml double cream**

**for the chocolate sauce:**
**200g dark chocolate, minimum 70%**
   **cocoa solids**

**14 bamboo skewers soaked in cold water**
   **to stop them catching fire in the heat of**
   **the barbecue or grill**

Preheat the grill or barbecue. Cut the top and bottom off the pineapple and, working vertically, slice the skin off the fruit. Cut into quarters and then into about three pieces again lengthways so that you have wedges of pineapple. Cut out the woody core and thread the wedges on to the soaked bamboo skewers lengthways and arrange these in a shallow dish.

Put the chocolate, broken up into pieces, into a thick-bottomed pan along with the Malibu and melt over a low heat. Then, stirring, pour in the cream, plus any juice that has gathered from the fruit. When the sauce is thick, smooth and hot, pour into a bowl with a ladle, or enough little bowls to give one per person.

Lay the pineapple kebabs on a sheet of foil and either grill or barbecue the pineapple, thickly coating it with demerara sugar first, until it caramelises and scorches in the heat.

Take off the barbecue and lay them on a large plate and let everyone take them as they want, dipping the pineapple skewers into the hot chocolate sauce as they eat.

Serves 6–8.

# BANANA AND BUTTERSCOTCH UPSIDE-DOWN TART

I normally have a firm rule: I don't write recipes for, or cook food, I don't absolutely love to eat myself; but I have to own up to a teensy little problem I have with cooked bananas. You might wonder why, then, I even bothered making this warm, gooey, caramel-sticky banana tart, but my sister requested it once and, as we all know, family life requires a tact and diplomacy that at times must overrule personal prejudice.

In truth, I did rather like it – but only straight out of the oven, before the bananas have time to cool to pungent mushiness. And in fact, you shouldn't leave it lying around wherever you stand on the cooked banana question: the pastry – which, before you start panicking, is bought – will become soggy if you don't eat it as soon as it's cooked. Not that this poses a problem: for the record, of all the puddings I've made for this book, this one was polished off fastest.

**375g ready-rolled butter puff pastry**
**50g unsalted butter**
**75g caster sugar**

**1 tablespoon golden syrup**
**1 tablespoon double cream**
**3–4 bananas**

Preheat the oven to 200°C/gas mark 6.

Cut a round of pastry, using a 20cm tarte tatin dish as your guide, and put in the fridge to use later.

Place the tarte tatin dish over a medium heat on the hob and melt the butter, then add the sugar, syrup and cream and whisk for a couple of minutes on the heat to make a thick butterscotch sauce.

Now, take this off the heat, and slice the bananas into 1cm thick rounds. Arrange the bananas in the slightly cooled sauce, and put the cut round of pastry over the top tucking the edges down well and sealing them so that the sauce cannot bubble up.

Bake for 20–25 minutes, by which time the pastry will have puffed up and turned golden brown. Take the dish out of the oven and place a plate over the top and very carefully turn the whole thing upside-down. The sight that meets you is a splendid one: the sauce-sticky, oven-blistered logs of banana forming a bronzey golden crown. And should any of these butterscotch-covered slices of banana be dislodged and stuck to the pan, don't get alarmed: just spatula them off and tuck them back in their rightful place. For absolute pleasure, eat with vanilla or coconut ice cream.

Serves 4–6.

# GINGERED AND MINTY FRUIT SALAD

I hesitate to give a recipe for fruit salad – by which I mean that there is no need to follow my instructions to the letter. Use the fruit you can find in whatever proportion pleases you. I find, in Middle-Eastern stores at any rate, you can get lychees and pomegranates in summer, but if you can't don't worry: consider some chunked watermelon instead. The ginger and mint in the syrup make this wonderfully refreshing; but don't worry, both these elements, along with the syrup in which they're infused, are light. I love this not just as a pudding, but for a late-morning summer's weekend breakfast – and at regular intervals during the day besides.

75ml water

45g caster sugar

3cm piece fresh ginger, peeled and roughly chopped

small palmful mint leaves, plus some for snipping over later

juice of half a lime

1 galia melon

1 honeydew melon

1 pawpaw

300g lychees, if available

2 white peaches

seeds from half a pomegranate, if available

Put the water and sugar in a tiny saucepan (I use one of those little copper ones made for melting butter in) and bring to the boil. Let boil for 5 minutes and while the syrup's bubbling away, put the chopped ginger and mint leaves in a small bowl or ramekin. When the five minutes are up, squeeze in the lime juice and then pour the syrup over the ginger and mint and let cool.

Then you can get on with the salad. For this you need two bowls, one for serving the fruit salad in and one for the detritus. Halve the melons, scoop the seeds into the non-serving bowl and using a melon-baller (please, indulge me) gouge out curvy pieces of melon. When the fruits are used up, squeeze the empty skins to get all the melon juice on to the pieces of fruit. Halve the pawpaw and scoop out the seeds into the detritus bowl and use the melon-baller to carve out more pieces of fruit, squeezing out the emptied skins as you did with the melons. Peel and stone the lychees and add these to the fruit bowl. Holding the peaches, one by one, over the rest of the fruit, cut out small segments and let them drop down over the rest of the fruit as you go.

Pour the cooled syrup into the detritus bowl and strain this over the fruit salad. Now add the pomegranate seeds. The best way of getting seeds out of a pomegranate is to hold a pomegranate half, seed side down, over the fruit bowl and then whack it with a wooden spoon. Nothing much will happen at first, but after a few thwacks, the seeds will rain down upon your salad most satisfyingly.

Chop a few mint leaves finely and scatter over. That's it.

Serves 6–8.

I don't think I could write a book that didn't include a recipe for trifle somewhere – and this, I tell you, is the trifle to end all trifles. The shiny black of the berries, the soft white-ness of the mascarpone above them and the golden toastiness of the almonds on top, make it, in the first instance, beautiful to look at. But the key element here is ease: unlike with other trifles, there is no caution-requiring cooking of custard, which however delicious, has its stresses. In fact, the only cooking whatsoever is a little heating of some jam on the stove. The Anglo factor is provided by the trifle sponges, jam and hedgerow-redolent fruit; the amaretti, limoncello – or any other lemon liqueur – and tiramisù-like eggy mascarpone layer fulfil the Italian side of the partnership.

I use blackcurrant rather than blackberry jam, simply because I want a more jel-lied, less pippy smearing between the sponges, but it wouldn't really matter which you go for. Similarly, feel free to use rum in place of the limoncello. It's just that I find it hard to come back from holiday in Italy without lugging strange lemon-shaped bottles of local liqueurs, and then want to justify the effort by finding some use for them in the kitchen.

As with all trifles, it's not the amounts which are so important, but the layering: in other words, different-sized bowls will require different quantities of ingredients; the ones that follow are enough to fill a bowl – and it should be glass – of about 2 litres capacity.

| | |
|---|---|
| **8 trifle sponges** | **750g blackberries** |
| **200g blackcurrant jam** | **2 eggs, separated** |
| **1 x 200g packet amaretti biscuits** | **100g caster sugar** |
| **250ml limoncello (or other lemon liqueur)** | **750g mascarpone cheese** |
| **juice of half a lemon** | **50g flaked almonds** |

Split the trifle sponges and make little sandwiches of them using 150g of the jam, then wodge them into the base of your glass bowl. Reduce the amaretti biscuits to rubble in the processor and, reserving some crumbs for sprinkling over the top at the end, scatter most of them evenly over the sponges and then pour over them 150ml of the limoncello. Put the remaining 50g of jam into a wide saucepan with the lemon juice and melt over a low heat, then tumble in the blackberries and turn in the heat for a minute or so just until the juices start running. Tip these over the biscuit-sprinkled, liqueur-soused sponge sand-wiches to cover and leave this while you get on with the next bit.

Whisk the egg yolks with the caster sugar until you have a thick smooth yellow paste. I use my Kitchen Aid for this, but any old hand-held electric mixer or whisk would be fine. Still whisking, drip in another 50ml limoncello and continue whisking away until you have a light moussey mixture. Whisk in the mascarpone until everything is smoothly combined, and when this is done add the remaining 50ml of limoncello. Finally, in another bowl, whisk the egg whites until firm, but not dry, and fold these into the lemony, eggy mascarpone mixture. Now spread this gently over the blackberries in the glass bowl.

Cover the thus-far assembled trifle with clingfilm and leave in the fridge for the flavours and textures to steep and meld for at least 4 hours and up to 24. Take the trifle out of the fridge for about 40 minutes to an hour before it's needed (depending on how cold your fridge runs) to get to coolish room temperature. Not long before you want to eat, toast the flaked almonds by tossing them in a dry, oil-less pan over medium heat until they are turning gold and flashed bronze in parts, then tip them on to a plate. When they're cool, mix them with the reserved amaretti crumbs. Remove the clingfilm from the bowl and scatter the nuts and crumbs over the pale, set surface. Dig in and serve, making sure to heap the full triple-banded layer on each plate: the lemony, almondy, cream-swathed berrieness makes this the perfect ending to a large, lazy summer lunch.

Serves 12–14.

This is so simple – scarcely a recipe really – but so good. Unless you get figs straight from the tree they sometimes need the blistering heat of an oven or grill to bring out all their honeyed sweetness. The cinnamon is emphatic, certainly, but it doesn't overwhelm the whole; it, rather, infuses the fruit, along with the kitchen you're cooking it in, with mellow spiciness. This is the pudding to end a slow-grazing, long-picking dinner eaten outside on a warm, balmy night.

If you haven't got any vanilla sugar, just use ordinary caster sugar and add a drop of pure vanilla extract along with the flower waters. A Middle-Eastern store of some kind will stock packets of slivered pistachios, vividly green and splintered into little boat-shaped shards. But if you can't get them, just buy shelled pistachios from a healthshop or supermarket and chop them roughly with a knife or mezzaluna yourself.

**12 black figs**
**50g unsalted butter**
**1 teaspoon ground cinnamon**
**1 tablespoon vanilla sugar**
**1 and a half teaspoons rosewater**

**1 and a half teaspoons orange-flower water**
**1 x 500g tub mascarpone cheese**
**100g slivered pistachio nuts**

Preheat a grill or oven to the fiercest it will go.

Quarter the figs, taking care not to cut all the way through to the bottom, so that they open like flowers, or young birds squawking to be fed worms by their mummy, and sit them, thus opened, in a heatproof dish into which they fit snugly.

Melt the butter in a small saucepan, then add the cinnamon, sugar and flower waters. Stir to combine and pour into the figs.

Blister under the hot grill or bake in the oven for a few minutes and then serve; it's that quick. Just give each person a couple of figs on a side plate. Splodge alongside some mascarpone over which you drizzle some of the conker-dark syrup, then sprinkle over some of those green, green shards of pistachio.

Serves 6.

# CHOCOLATE PEANUT SQUARES

There is something, particularly in the heat, about the combination of salty and sweet. In truth this is nothing more than an elaboration of millionaire's shortbread, suggested to me by a Saturday night spent lying in bed watching *The Bone Collector* on TV while eating clumps of peanuts out of my left hand and slabs of chocolate from my right. Who wouldn't be inspired by that heavenly mingle in the mouth? Ambrosia from the Gods.

**for the shortbread base:**
225g plain flour
75g caster sugar
175g soft unsalted butter

**for the peanut filling:**
200g soft butter
1 x 397g tin condensed milk
4 tablespoons golden syrup
250g dry-roasted salted peanuts

**for the topping:**
250g good-quality dark chocolate
  (70% cocoa solids)
75g good-quality milk chocolate
  (or 325g dark chocolate alone, to taste)

23cm square brownie tin or similar,
sides and bottom lined with baking
  parchment

Preheat the oven to 160°C/gas mark 3.

Make the shortbread base the agreeably lazy way by dumping the flour, sugar and butter into the bowl of a food processor fitted with the double-bladed knife, and process until you have a sandy mixture that is beginning to clump up. Turn this out on to the lined tin and press the mixture in with your fingers. If you have long nails you may find this easier, or at least more cleanly achieved, by using the back of a spoon. Once the mixture's all pressed in, smooth it either with your hands or a spatula. Prick it at regular intervals with a fork and cook it in the preheated oven for 5 minutes, then lower the oven to 150°C/gas mark 2, and cook for a further 30–40 minutes until it is a pale gold and no longer doughy. Remove to a wire rack and let cool in the tin.

For the peanut-caramel filling, spoon the 200g butter into a large microwave-able bowl and melt in the microwave – this should take 2–3 minutes – then add the condensed milk and golden syrup. Whisk the mixture well until everything is combined and stick the bowl back into the microwave. Cook on medium for 6–7 minutes until it is boiling, removing it very gingerly every couple of minutes to give it a good stir. (Making the caramel in the microwave this way is much quicker than the traditional method, and the way I always do it, but be careful not to burn yourself. One day I'll show you my battle scars.) It's ready when the gooey mixture has thickened and turned a light, golden brown. Stand to cool for a minute or so and then whisk a bit to disperse the heat. Stir in the dry-roasted peanuts then pour and scrape over the cooled shortbread, spreading with a rubber spatula to make sure it's evenly covered, and leave it to set.

Again, I always use a microwave to melt chocolate: it is quite the easiest way – no faffing with bowls suspended over pans of simmering water – and the chocolate melts smoothly and seems much less likely to seize. Just break the chocolate into pieces into a microwaveable bowl and cook on medium for a couple of minutes; after which time it may need another couple before it's melted, but it's better to take this slowly. Out of the microwave, give the melted chocolate a slow stir with a rubber spatula to combine both milk or dark (leave it alone if using dark only), and pour and spread it (remembering that the less you touch it, the shinier it will be) over the peanutty caramel mixture in the tin. Leave it to cool.

Once set, cut the chocolate peanut block into 24 squares. If you are foolhardy enough to have arranged a picnic, make sure you bring a batch of these along. Just pack the tin, along with a good knife, and cut on site.

Makes 24 squares.

# WHITE CHOCOLATE AND PASSIONFRUIT MOUSSE

So much in cooking, as in the rest of life I suppose, is about contrast, about balance. Here the acerbic fragrance of the passionfruit undercuts the otherwise over-egged richness of the white chocolate: this gives you flavour, intensity, sweetness *and* light.

On standing, the clear, sour-sweet juices of the fruit collect under the mousse: place raspberries in the glass first (again contrast, this time of colour, too) and let them become plumply infused and almost headily soused beneath.

**300g white chocolate**

**6 eggs, separated**

**10 passionfruit**

**300–500g raspberries**

Break the chocolate into pieces and melt in the microwave for about 3 minutes, or in a bowl over a pan of simmering water (and see remarks on melting white chocolate on page 214) then set the bowl aside, and let the chocolate cool a little.

Beat the egg whites until stiff but not dry. Mix the egg yolks into the cooled chocolate, though be gentle to ensure it doesn't seize. Cut the passionfruit in half and scoop them, juice, pulp, seeds, into the yolk and chocolate mixture, then fold into the egg whites until completely incorporated.

Line the bottom of either a big glass bowl or eight to ten small glasses with a layer of raspberries – it's hard to be specific: it depends on the diameter of the glasses, or bowl, at the base really – and pour over the mousse. Leave for a couple of hours to set in the fridge, or for at least 4 if you're using one large bowl. Strangely, given that I lean normally towards the communal rather than individual serving, I generally go the one-glass-one-person route. I think it's because this is intense enough to require – even for me – small portions, and it's impossible to dollop out as little as would fill a small glass without seeming mean.

Serves 8–10.

# COCONUT SLAB

I have a weakness for army-style catering: the bigger the pan, the happier I am, and there is something particularly satisfying about baking a cake in a roasting pan. This is my regular for the cake stall at the school summer fete, but those whose lives are serenely untouched by the demands of the PTA can wheel it out, with an easily assembled salad of roughly chunked papaya, mango, pineapple and spooned-out passionfruit, dressed with a squeeze or two of lime, to provide a Beano-portioned pudding for expansive parties on hot summer days or to produce atmosphere of same.

*for the cake:*
**350g soft unsalted butter**
**350g caster sugar**
**6 eggs**
**400g self-raising flour (or plain flour
    with 3–4 teaspoons baking powder)**
**50g cornflour**
**1 teaspoon coconut essence**
**100g creamed coconut cut from a slab
    put into a measuring jug and filled up
    to the 300ml mark with freshly boiled
    water**

*for the icing:*
**1kg icing sugar, sieved**
**approx. 150ml milk**
**30g unsalted butter**
**1 teaspoon coconut essence**
**6–8 tablespoons desiccated coconut to
    sprinkle (optional)**

**33 x 24 x 6cm tin or roasting pan, sides
    and bottom lined with baking
    parchment**

Preheat the oven to 180°C/gas mark 4.

I make this coconut sponge in the Kitchen Aid mixer, but use whatever method you want. Just cream the butter and sugar first, until pale and light, then beat in one egg at a time, after which dollop in, bit by bit after each egg, the flour mixed with the cornflour. When all is combined, stir in the coconut essence. While you've been doing this the creamed coconut should have melted in the water to form a liquid; give it a quick whisk and beat it into the batter. It will be a fairly runny mix, so be prepared to pour rather than scrape into the lined tin.

Bake for 45 minutes or until the sponge is springy and coming away at the sides. Sit the tin on a wire rack for about 20 minutes and then turn out on to the rack to cool.

Once it's cool, you can get on with the icing, which is a simple enough affair. Melt all the ingredients except the desiccated coconut in a saucepan over low to medium heat, stirring every now and again with a wooden spoon, and when you have a cohesive, gleaming mixture, all butter melted, pour it over the top of the cake. The icing should be thick enough to cover the top in a smooth white blanket and not dribble off the sides, so add more milk or icing sugar if it's either too thick or too runny. Sprinkle the desiccated coconut on top of the cake – if you care to – while the icing is still slightly wet. And, for maximum aesthetic pleasure, leave this slab whole and uncut, iced and almost blindingly, totally mesmerically white, like summer snow, until you actually serve it.

Makes 24 squares.

# GOOSEBERRY FOOL

I love the acid tang of gooseberries, all the more desirable for being one of the few remaining seasonal ingredients, against the mouth-cooling, aerated blandness of the cream. On top of which, it's simple, comforting, elegant: what more do you want from food? As a combination, it's hard to beat. I don't think it does to play around with this sort of thing generally, but a tablespoon of elderflower cordial (for those of us who don't have access to the real thing) added to the cream is a respectful innovation, if indeed it is that; the conjunction of elderflower and gooseberry was a favoured one of the Victorians, who knew a thing or two about puddings (and see the recipe for gooseberry and elderflower ice cream on page 233).

I haven't been specific about the amount of sugar used, but that's because gooseberries tend to differ enormously in their respective sourness or sweetness, and obviously if you are using the elderflower cordial you will already be adding sugar in another guise.

**500g gooseberries**
**60g butter**
**caster sugar to taste**

**300ml double or whipping cream**
**1 tablespoon elderflower cordial**
 **(optional)**

Top and tail the gooseberries. Melt the butter in a large pan and add the fruit. Cover and turn the heat down to low and let them cook gently for about 5 minutes. When their greenness has softened to mushy yellow, take the pan off the heat and squish the fruit more with a wooden spoon, or give a quick go with a whisk. Don't mash to a purée, though: you want some texture. Taste and, as I've said, add sugar as you think the mashed gooseberries need it: it depends on how young they are, how freshly cooked, and on your palate. Put the fruit in a bowl and leave it to cool.

Whip the cream till softly peaking – you don't want it too stiff – and then fold in the fruit. If you're using it, add the elderflower cordial. But mix gently: you want the cream to be punctuated by the sharp fruit, not all one pulpy mass.

I like this better in one bowl rather than in individual glasses, but it's up to you.

Serves 4–6.

# CHOCOLATE RASPBERRY PAVLOVA

You just cannot beat a pav in summer, and in particular this dark beauty. The crisp and chewy chocolate meringue base, rich in cocoa and beaded nuggets of chopped plain chocolate, provides a sombre, almost purple-brown layer beneath the fat whiteness of the cream and matt, glowering crimson raspberries on top: it is a killer combination.

| | |
|---|---|
| *for the chocolate meringue base:* | *for the topping:* |
| **6 egg whites** | **500ml double cream** |
| **300g caster sugar** | **500g raspberries** |
| **3 tablespoons cocoa powder, sieved** | **2–3 tablespoons coarsely grated dark** |
| **1 teaspoon balsamic or red wine vinegar** | **chocolate** |
| **50g dark chocolate, finely chopped** | |

Preheat the oven to 180°C/gas mark 4 and line a baking tray with baking parchment.

Beat the egg whites until satiny peaks form, and then beat in the sugar a spoonful at a time until the meringue is stiff and shiny. Sprinkle over the cocoa and vinegar, and the chopped chocolate. Then gently fold everything until the cocoa is thoroughly mixed in. Mound on to a baking sheet in a fat circle approximately 23cm in diameter, smoothing the sides and top. Place in the oven, then immediately turn the temperature down to 150°C/gas mark 2 and cook for about one to one and a quarter hours. When it's ready it should look crisp around the edges and on the sides and be dry on top, but when you prod the centre you should feel the promise of squidginess beneath your fingers. Turn off the oven and open the door slightly, and let the chocolate meringue disc cool completely.

When you're ready to serve, invert on to a big, flat-bottomed plate. Whisk the cream till thick but still soft and pile it on top of the meringue, then scatter over the raspberries. Coarsely grate the chocolate so that you get curls rather than rubble, as you don't want the raspberries' luscious colour and form to be obscured, and sprinkle haphazardly over the top, letting some fall, as it will, on the plate's rim.

Serves 8–10.

# PASSIONFRUIT PAVLOVA, AGAIN

I hesitate before reprinting a recipe I've published before but after writing about the chocolate pavlova on the previous page, I couldn't resist a quick return to the passion-fruit pavlova in *How To Eat*. It's just that, in all honesty, I couldn't contemplate a summer without it. There is something about the mixture between sugary marshmallow-bellied meringue, soft cream and pippy, fragrantly astringent fruit that works too well for me to ignore it now.

Follow the method for the meringue base on the previous page, using 4 egg whites, 250g caster sugar, 2 teaspoons cornflour (which you add as you do the cocoa), and a teaspoon of white vinegar along with a few drops of pure vanilla extract. Mound into a 21cm round on the parchment-lined baking sheet and put into the same, 180°C/gas mark 4 oven, turning the heat down immediately to 150°C/gas mark 2, cooking exactly as for the chocolate version. Once cooled, invert likewise, this time covering with 300ml of whipped double cream and the juicy pulp of 10 scooped-out passionfruits; this slightly smaller pav will feed 6–8.

# MINT CHOCOLATE MOUSSE

I've tried this mousse a number of different ways and I've come to the conclusion that it tastes best when made with the best quality mint chocolate. I must own up that this makes it a pretty expensive proposition: Ackerman's hand-made, plain chocolate mint wafers don't come cheap. But any good dark mint chocolate works well, as long as the mint is infused in the chocolate rather than a white, creamy filling within it. If you can find really good-quality peppermint oil, though, you're away: just use a few drops along with the best, plain chocolate you can find. And the mint does make a difference, you know: it turns this from a comfort-food, wintry bistro-pud into a musky, intense hit of smooth summer richness.

Not that I'm claiming any originality here: this is about as traditional a combination as you can get; but somehow, its deep unfashionableness and cool heat make it fresh.

**300g mint chocolate**              **2 tablespoons caster sugar**
**30g soft unsalted butter**         **few leaves fresh mint**
**6 eggs**

Break the chocolate into pieces into a bowl, add the butter and put into the microwave, on medium, for 3–4 minutes, though check after 2 to be on the safe side. When the chocolate's melted set the bowl aside to let it cool a little. Separate the eggs and put the yolks and sugar into one bowl; in another, whisk the egg whites until you have a stiff – but not dry – snow, and set aside.

Now beat the yolks and sugar together then pour, and fold, into the cooled chocolate. When fully combined, add a quarter of the beaten egg whites and vigorously beat to incorporate fully. Now go more gently as you add further dollops of the egg whites and fold them into the chocolate base. When all the whites are folded in, pour into a glass bowl (or four to six individual glasses if you prefer), cover with clingfilm, and chill in the fridge for a good 4 hours, though longer's fine. And don't be self-conscious: decorate the centre of the bowl with a few leaves of mint, or place one or two on top of each little mousse in its glass, before serving. You know you want to.

Serves 4–6.

There is a hint of the days-gone-by sweet trolley about this: it's not as tricksy to make as the *arance alla principessa* I remember from my childhood, the pudding I always chose on treaty weekend jaunts with my grandparents to the now defunct San Marino in Connaught Street, but rather a rougher-hewn, contemporarily pared down and more huskily aromatic version of the same.

I love these oranges really cold, crispy with caramel and richly dolloped with Greek yoghurt, which means you need to make them enough in advance so that they've got time to chill in the fridge. But don't make them too far in advance: after a day, the sugary carapace will disappear, melting into the fruit's juices.

**6 navel oranges or any small thin-skinned variety**

**500g caster sugar**

**250ml water**

**8 cardamom pods, crushed**

**Greek yoghurt (approx. 500g)**

Using a small sharp knife, cut a thin slice off the top and bottom of the oranges, and then slice off the skin vertically, turning the orange as you go, being careful to keep as much flesh as possible but removing all pith.

Slice each orange into 5mm rounds, trying to reserve as much juice as you can. Just plonk the slices, pouring the juices, into a bowl as you cut them. Or just cut them straight into something like a lasagne dish.

To make the caramel, put the sugar, water and cardamom pods into a large saucepan and swirl (*not* stir) a little to dissolve the sugar. Then slowly bring to the boil without stirring, until the syrup becomes a dark amber colour.

Take the saucepan off the heat and tip in the oranges and any juice that's collected in the bowl. Quickly coat the orange slices in the caramel and pour on to a flat plate; act with speed otherwise the caramel will set before you can get it out of the saucepan. If you can pick out the cardamom pods without burning your fingers, great, but there's no need to get too exercised about it: let those eating do a little work as well.

Let the oranges cool, and then put them in the fridge to chill for a little while. Put the Greek yoghurt in a bowl on the table for people to eat it with.

Serves 6–8.

# LEMON RICE PUDDING

There is nothing I can do here: you either love rice pudding or hate it; only you know which. Having said that, this is a rice pudding far removed from school-dinner hell: it's cool, skinless, infused with lemon and lightened with softly whipped double cream. Decant it into individual glasses and eat almost like a lemon-rice fool, or serve out of one huge bowl. I like it pale, undecorated, unaccompanied, just as it is, though it certainly goes very well with blueberries, providing you can find ones that actually taste of blueberries. If you're going the individually portioned route, tumble a pile of berries into the glass first and dollop the rice on top.

Towards the end of summer, or when it's passed, when you might want to inject a little warmth into supper, serve alongside a dish of roast plums. Use any colour you want, for taste, but those fiery red ones look ludicrously magnificent: just cut each plum in half, remove the stones, place the plums to sit snugly in a buttered ovenproof dish, sprinkle a little sugar in each cavity and blitz in a hot oven, around 200°C/gas mark 6, for 20 minutes or so.

**100g pudding rice**
**zest of 2 lemons and juice of 1**
**1 litre full-fat milk**

**3 tablespoons caster sugar**
**250ml double cream**
**few drops lemon oil**

Put the pudding rice, lemon zest and milk into a wide-bottomed saucepan and bring to the boil over medium heat. As soon as the milk's started bubbling, turn the heat right down and, if you've got one, put a heat diffuser underneath the pan; the more slowly you cook the rice, the more gloriously creamy it is. To stop the rice forming a skin – and I shudder even to mention the word – cover the milk directly with a piece of greaseproof paper. I will try and explain how I do this: I cut out a large square – slightly bigger than the circumference of the pan – and then fold all four corners in, rather as if I were making a kite, not that I've ever done such a thing in my life. Then I sit this piece of paper on top of the milk and rice in the pan and fold the corners back out so that they stick to the interior of the pan, above the milk. Let the rice cook like this for about 40 minutes, or until the rice is cooked and most of the liquid absorbed (the milk will continue being absorbed as the rice cools). Take the rice off the heat and beat in the sugar, then leave to stand for 5 minutes or so before beating in the juice of the lemon; if the rice is too hot, it will curdle as you do this. If you want you can use a few drops of lemon oil in place of the juice here; at any rate, you will be needing it later.

Turn the rice pudding into a bowl and, performing your kite-folding trick again, cover with greaseproof paper. Leave to cool, and then chill in the fridge. Once it's really cold, take it out of the fridge, remove its paper lid and then whip the cream with a few drops of lemon oil until thick but not clumping and stiff, and fold into the rice pudding.

Serves 8–10.

# LEMON CUPCAKES

I cannot resist, either in the making or the eating, a cupcake, and this is the perfect sunshine version, to be taken on picnics or eaten at home. Yes, I know the little jelly lemon halves that adorn the tops are fake and plasticky, but that is part of their charm. And you can find them, along with the lemon oil and the instant royal icing, at the baking aisle at most supermarkets.

**250g self-raising flour**
**250g very soft unsalted butter**
**250g caster sugar**
**4 eggs**
**1 teaspoon lemon oil**
**2–3 tablespoons milk to bind**

*for the icing:*
**1 x 500g packet Instant Royal Icing**
  **powder**
**juice of 1 large lemon**
**24 lemon jelly slices**

Preheat the oven to 200°C/gas mark 6 and line a couple of 12-bun cupcake or muffin tins with paper cases. Take butter, eggs and milk out of the fridge in time to make sure they're at room temperature.

Put all the ingredients for the cupcakes, except for the milk, into the bowl of a food processor, fitted with the double-bladed knife, and blitz till totally combined. Process again, adding enough milk to make a batter with a smooth, flowing texture, then remove the blade and spoon and scrape the batter equally into the waiting cupcake cases. Remember the cakes rise as they bake: there is enough mixture to fill each case adequately even if you panic when you first look at it.

Bake for about 20 minutes, by which time the sponge should be cooked through and springy to the touch. Remove from the oven, leave for 5 minutes or so and then arrange the cupcakes in their paper cases on a couple of wire racks to cool.

Once they're cool, you can get on with the icing. Just whisk the instant royal icing with the lemon juice (using a free-standing mixer or electric whisk) until thick and smooth: you want the icing to sit thickly on the cupcakes not run off them. And you can aid this by cutting off any risen humps with a sharp knife first, so each cake is flat-topped, though be careful if you're icing over any cut surface: you want no crumbs dislodged and left to besmirch the pale, sugary smoothness of the topping. I like the icing coolly white like this, but if you don't mind an E-additive or two, and want to go out for full on sun, then add a drop of yellow food colouring as you make up the icing. No purist stance is intended here: after all, I now require you to top each cupcake with a miniature, sugar-jelly slice of lemon.

Makes 24.

# LAVENDER TRUST CUPCAKES

There was a fashion, some time ago, for lavender-scented custards and creams. I always resisted it. But I made these a while ago, for auction to raise money for the Lavender Trust, which is the charity for young women with breast cancer, set up in memory of Ruth Picardie, and – you know – the lavender works: it immediately evokes the musky scent of summer without filling the mouth with soapy perfume. Of course, in Provence, lavender is routinely used in the most savoury of cooking, much as rosemary is, but I have yet to embrace my inner Peter Mayle. This, though, may be my first small step. To make lavender sugar, just cut up a few lavender sprigs and keep them in a jar of caster sugar for a few days. Or you can buy it, in jars, ready concocted; a company called Hanbury make a number of flavoured sugars.

| | |
|---|---|
| **125g self-raising flour** | **for the icing:** |
| **125g very soft unsalted butter** | **approx. 250g Instant Royal Icing** |
| **125g lavender sugar, sieved** | **violet icing colour** |
| **2 eggs** | **handful of real lavender stalks** |
| **pinch salt** | |
| **few tablespoons milk** | |

Preheat the oven to 200°C/gas mark 6, line a 12-bun muffin tin with paper cases and get butter, eggs and milk out of the fridge in time to get to room temperature before you start.

Make the cupcakes as usual: put all the cake ingredients, bar the milk, into the processor and combine, adding milk to bind. Using spoon and rubber spatula, fill the cake-cases equally and bake for 20 minutes or so, until cooked (see page 195).

Cool the cupcakes as for the lemon cupcakes, and slice off any humped tops. Make up the icing according to packet instructions, dyeing the mixture a faint lilac with a spot or two of food colouring: I like to use the solid pastes for which you may have to go to a specialist cake decoration shop, I'm afraid; the colour you'll want here is generally labelled 'grape violet'. Go carefully, though: we want pastel serenity here, not Seventies record-sleeve murk.

Top each pretty-pale cupcake with a little sprig of lavender before the icing's set dry.

Makes 12.

You might think that no recipe could live up to this title. It's a reasonable presumption, but thank God, a wrong one. This is heaven on the plate: the wine-soused raspberries take on a stained glass, lucent red, their very raspberriness enhanced; the soft, translucently pale coral just-set jelly in which they sit has a heady, floral fragrance that could make a grateful eater weep. If there's one pudding you make from this book, please, please make it this.

This recipe was emailed to me from Australia from my erstwhile editor, Eugenie Boyd. I've fiddled with it a bit, but it is the best present a foodwriter could ever have. Now it's yours.

**1 bottle good fruity Chardonnay**　　　　**5 gelatine leaves**
**300g raspberries**　　　　**250g caster sugar**
**1 vanilla pod, split lengthways**　　　　**double cream to serve**

Place the wine and berries in a bowl and allow to steep for half an hour. Strain the wine into a saucepan and keep the raspberries to one side. Heat the wine with the vanilla pod until nearly boiling and leave to steep on one side for 15 minutes.

Soak the gelatine leaves – which you can find in the supermarket these days – in cold water for about 5 minutes. Meanwhile, after removing the vanilla pod, reheat the wine and stir in the sugar until it dissolves; allow to boil if you want to lose the alcohol. Add a third of the hot wine to the wrung-out gelatine leaves in a measuring jug and stir to dissolve, then add this mixture back into the rest of the wine and stir well. Strain into a large jug.

Place the raspberries, equally, into six flattish, clear glass serving bowls, and pour the strained wine over the top.

Allow to set in the fridge for at least 3 hours, though a day would be fine if you want to make this well ahead, and take out of the fridge 15 minutes before serving.

Serve some double cream in a jug, and let people pour this into the fragrant, tender, fruit-jewelled jelly as they eat.

Serves 6.

# ORANGE CORNMEAL CAKE

This is one of those slightly Italianate cakes in form, by which I mean it is intentionally shallow and unspongey. It's meant to be eaten, cut into wedges, as pudding – and the cornmeal makes it crumble deliciously into a cream and berry lined spoon. In fact, summer always needs plain, unshowy cakes like these: the perfect vehicle for red-glowing seasonal fruit. Orange itself is hardly associated exclusively with summer, indeed far from it, but its flavour seems to make any berry more intense. For this reason, in deep midwinter, I add the grated zest of an orange to a plate of frozen summer berries as they thaw; serve them thus, with this cake, whenever mood calls for a little summer lightness and the produce in the shops will not oblige.

You can get the orange oil at most supermarkets these days, but if you can't get hold of some just add more zest. It won't give such a pronounced orange flavour, but it will still be good.

**250g soft unsalted butter**

**125g fine (yellow) cornmeal, plus some for lining tin**

**175g caster sugar**

**4 eggs**

**60ml plain yoghurt**

**zest of 1 orange, juice of half**

**half teaspoon orange oil**

**50g plain flour**

**1 and a half teaspoons baking powder**

*to serve:*

**raspberries, or mixed summer berries, and crème fraîche, mascarpone or whipped double cream**

Preheat the oven to 180°C/gas mark 4.

Butter a 23cm Springform tin and line it with baking parchment, shake some cornmeal into the tin and let it stick to the sides and bottom. Tap out any excess.

Using an electric mixer for ease, beat the butter until light and add the sugar. Beat in the eggs one at a time, followed by the yoghurt, orange juice then zest and orange oil. Fold in the cornmeal, flour and baking powder and blend everything together well before pouring into the Springform tin.

Bake for about 40 minutes or until the top is golden brown and springs back when pressed lightly with your finger.

Let it cool slightly on a rack before springing the tin open and letting the cake cool completely.

Serves 8–10 with the generous addition of berries and cream or mascarpone.

# EASTERN MEDITERRANEAN CHEESECAKE

To be true to this cheesecake's provenance, you would be using kaymak, a rich, creamy curd cheese made of buffalo milk; I've let you off with a mixture of curd cheese, cream cheese and soured cream instead. Does this make it authentic? I don't know: but it is authentically good. For me that's enough. I make no claims other than that.

This is not a cheesecake as one might usually expect: there is no biscuit base, no base of any sort indeed; and the taste and texture is similarly different: there's not that melting, mouth-filling richness, but something altogether lighter and more flutteringly fragrant. The whisked egg whites give it a delicate almost-moussiness; the orange-flower water, honey and cinnamon provide a light aromatic tang. It needs no accompaniment: serve just as it is.

**50g soft unsalted butter**
**100g caster sugar**
**1 tablespoon plain flour**
**250g curd cheese**
**250g cream cheese**
**150ml soured cream**

**2 tablespoons orange-blossom honey**
**5 eggs, separated**
**1 tablespoon orange-flower water**
**1 teaspoon ground cinnamon**
**1 tablespoon caster sugar**
**2–3 tablespoons flaked almonds**

Preheat the oven to 160°C/gas mark 3. Butter and line a 23cm Springform tin.

Cream together the butter and the sugar until light and fluffy, with the instrument of your choice (mine's a Kitchen Aid; a hand-held electric whisk would be fine), then add the flour. Gently beat in the curd and cream cheeses and the soured cream, and then the honey and egg yolks. Finally add the orange-flower water.

In a separate bowl, whisk the egg whites until they are stiff but not dry, and fold them into the cheese mixture. Pour into the tin, and then dust the top with the cinnamon and caster sugar and then sprinkle over the flaked almonds.

Cook in the oven for an hour – it will rise up and crack but that's just what it does – then turn the oven off and leave the cake in there for another hour, and it will sink back into the tin.

Take the cheesecake out of the oven and let cool in the tin on a wire rack, before springing it open when you want to eat it.

Serves 6–8.

This is another Oz-emanating recipe, one I scribbled down from a friend once after a gardenside, Sunday's summer lunch. And you should know that I have never made it myself without some other friend asking me, in turn, for the recipe as well. Pavlova meets Victoria sponge is, give or take, what it is: but, as lazy luck would have it, much simpler to make than that or its ceremonious title would suggest.

| | |
|---|---|
| **125g plain flour** | **2 teaspoons pure vanilla extract** |
| **25g cornflour** | **2 tablespoons milk** |
| **1 and a half teaspoons baking powder** | **50g flaked almonds** |
| **100g very soft unsalted butter** | **375ml double cream** |
| **300g caster sugar** | **250g strawberries** |
| **4 eggs** | |

Preheat the oven to 200°C/gas mark 6. Line, butter and flour 2 x 22cm Springform tins.

Weigh out the flour, cornflour and baking powder into a bowl.

Cream the butter and 100g of the caster sugar in another bowl until light and fluffy. Separate the eggs and beat the yolks into the butter and sugar, saving the whites to whisk later. Gently fold in the weighed-out dry ingredients, add the vanilla, and then stir in the milk to thin the batter. Divide the mixture between the two prepared Springform tins.

Whisk the egg whites until soft peaks form, then gradually add the remaining 200g caster sugar. Spread a layer of meringue on top of the sponge batter in each tin, and sprinkle the almonds evenly over.

Bake for 30–35 minutes, by which time the top of the almond-scattered meringues will be a dark gold. Let the cakes cool in their tins, then spring them open at the last minute when you are ready to assemble the cake.

Whip the double cream, and hull and slice the strawberries; that's to say, the bigger ones can be sliced lengthways and the smaller ones halved. Invert one of the cakes on to a plate or cakestand so that the sponge is uppermost. Pile on the cream and stud with the strawberries, letting some of the berries subside into the whipped whiteness. Place the second cake on top, meringue upwards, and press down gently, just to secure it.

If you've got any more strawberries in the house, hull and halve them, and serve them in a dish on a table to eat alongside; it gives the cake a more after-lunch, less afternoon-tea kind of a feel, but it's hardly obligatory.

Serves 8.

This is old-fashioned, nostalgia-perfect English summer in pudding form: vanilla-scented, rhubarb-rippled, totally dreamy.

Make sure you use the rosiest, reddest rhubarb you can: that monster stuff, dredged up almost khaki at the very end of August, will not quite do here. I don't want to anger the nation's greengrocers, but I've found Marks & Spencer's sell rhubarb that is reliably pink all the year around. And it's hardly seasonal to mention it, but of course the purest, pucest stalks are the forced kind that fill the shops after Christmas: no matter, you will want to eat this whenever you can.

If you haven't got any vanilla sugar to hand (though you can have, just by leaving a vanilla pod or two in a jar of caster sugar for a few days, even less if you cut the pod up), use ordinary caster sugar and add a teaspoon of pure vanilla extract to the cream when you whip it. This recipe is not Simon Hopkinson's but is wholly, chest-swellingly inspired by it.

I deviate sometimes from it in the summer months – actually, throughout the year, now I come to think of it – by following exactly the same rhubarb-cooking method, but instead of doing anything with it further, I serve it simply as it is, roasted to tender pinkness, to be eaten still warm, with egg-custard ice cream (and see page 224). Or just use a tub of good shop-bought vanilla instead.

**1kg rhubarb, trimmed and coarsely chopped**

**300g vanilla sugar**

**500ml double cream**

Preheat the oven to 190°C/gas mark 5.

Mix the rhubarb and vanilla sugar together in an ovenproof dish. Do not add water. Cover with foil and bake for 45 minutes to 1 hour or until the fruit is completely soft. Drain in a colander, or sieve, and pour the juice (you should have about 500ml) into a saucepan, then heat and let bubble away until reduced by about half. Pour into a jug and leave to cool; do not, however, refrigerate as the syrup might crystallise and lose its fabulous puce clarity. Purée the fruit until totally smooth, then cool and chill this as well.

Whip the cream in a large chilled bowl until lusciously thick but not stiff. Carefully fold in the rhubarb purée, then some of the reduced juice, so the mixture is streaked, rather like raspberry ripple ice cream. Put the juice in a glass jug so that people can add more, if they want, as they eat. Or frankly, you could instead use half the amount of rhubarb juice in the pan for reducing and use the remaining 250ml for adding to champagne for a fabulous, blush-pink summer drink.

I know that the saying goes that you cannot improve on perfection, but just make a batch of vanilla shortbread (see page 207) to go with . . .

Serves 8.

# VANILLA SHORTBREAD

I know that biscuits sound like the sort of cooking someone else does, but you need never have baked anything ever in your life to be able to make these with untroubled ease. And I hate to say this – as someone with a once-serious Bahlsen habit – but they are so much better than anything out of a packet.

**100g icing sugar**
**200g plain flour, preferably Italian 00**
**100g cornflour**
**200g very soft unsalted butter**

**seeds from 1 vanilla pod**
**vanilla or ordinary caster sugar for**
  **sprinkling**

Preheat the oven to 160°C/gas mark 3.

Put the icing sugar, plain flour and cornflour into the bowl of a food processor fitted with the double-bladed knife and give them a quick blitz (just to save you sieving, which is my most-hated job in the kitchen) before adding the butter along with the vanilla seeds you've scraped out of a pod. (I find the easiest way to do this is by cutting the pod in half across, and then splitting each short half lengthwise and prising out the seeds with the point and edge of a sharp knife. Don't even think of throwing the deseeded bits of pod away: stash them in a jar of caster to use next time a recipe requires vanilla sugar.)

Process again until the soft mixture coheres and begins to form a ball, loosely clumping around the blade. Turn this out on to a Swiss roll tin and press to form an even (or as even as you can make it) layer, using fingers or the back of a spoon, or both. Be patient: I promise you it will fit smoothly.

Using the tip of a sharp knife cut the pressed-out shortbread into fingers. I make two incisions lengthways – ie to form three layers – and then make ten cuts down – so that you end up with eleven fingers per layer. Obviously, the aim should be to cut at regular intervals but don't start getting your ruler out. Just go by eye: uniformity is the province of the conveyer belt not of home cooking. Use the tines of a fork to make little holes in each marked-out biscuit: I press down about three times, diagonally, on each finger.

Now that you've pressed, incised, and punctured, slide the Swiss roll tin into the oven and bake for about 20–25 minutes, by which time the shortbread will be pale still, but not doughy. Expect a little goldenness around the edges, but shortbread should be not crisp but melting. Remove the tin from the oven and let cool for 10 minutes or so, before removing, with a palette knife and your fingers, to a wire rack. Sprinkle with sugar and leave them to cool completely before storing in a tin.

Makes 33 fingers.

# PASSIONFRUIT SHORTCAKES

Shortcakes are one of America's great culinary contributions, somewhere between sponge cake and scone, over there sandwiched with (often) sweetened cream and strawberries, but I love them too like this, Oz-style: the cream softly whipped and innocent of vanilla or sugar, and with almost astringently aromatic passionfruit scooped out on top. It's the perfect ending to a garden-fragrant summer lunch.

A more Anglo-version, to be eaten on an idyll of a blue-skied afternoon, replaces the scooped-out passionfruit with rubied dollops of hands-free, home-made fresh raspberry jam. This is so simple, so effortless and so summery, that I have to reprise the recipe, quickly, from *How To Be A Domestic Goddess*: put 250g raspberries into one ovenproof dish and 250g caster sugar into another (a flat, round pie-dish shape is best). Cook both in an oven preheated to 180°C/gas mark 4 for 20–25 minutes, then remove from the oven and add the hot sugar to the hot berries. As you do so, so your jam is made, an instant, molten, red-gleaming river of it. Pour into a 250ml jar and leave to cool and set before storing in the fridge. Spoon out on to cream-clouded shortcakes, as suggested – or eat any way pleasure suggests.

325g plain flour
half a teaspoon salt
1 tablespoon baking powder
5 tablespoons caster sugar
125g unsalted butter, frozen
1 large egg, beaten

125ml single cream
1 egg white, lightly beaten

*for the filling:*
250ml double cream
3 large passionfruit (or 6 small)

Preheat the oven to 200°C/gas mark 6.

Sift the flour, salt and baking powder into a large bowl and add 3 tablespoons of the sugar. Grate the butter into these dry ingredients, and use your fingertips to finish crumbling the butter into the flour. All you need to do is use the coarse holes of an ordinary grater, but if you prefer just cut the butter into pea-sized pieces and work it into the flour either by hand or with the paddle attachment of a free-standing mixer.

Whisk the egg into the single cream, and pour into the flour mixture a little at a time, using a fork to mix. You may not need all of the eggy cream to make the dough come together, so go cautiously.

Turn the dough out on to a lightly floured surface, and roll lightly to a thickness of about 2cm. Using a 6.5cm round scone or biscuit cutter, dipped in flour, cut out as many rounds as you can. Work the scraps back into a dough and re-roll if necessary to form six rounds in all.

Place the shortcakes about 2.5cm apart on a baking sheet, brush the tops with the egg white, and sprinkle them with the remaining 2 tablespoons of caster sugar. (If it helps with the rest of your cooking, or life in general, you can cover and refrigerate them now for up to 2 hours.) Bake for 10-15 minutes, until golden brown, and let them cool for a short while on a wire rack. The shortcakes should be eaten while still warm, so this stage doesn't take that long. But don't panic if they aren't warm when you eat them; the one thing you don't want to be doing is hovering nervously about the oven when you've got friends over.

Either before you sit down to eat or as you go to assemble the shortcakes, whichever suits you best, whip the double cream until floppily thick. Just before you want to bring them out, split each shortcake across the middle, dollop some of the softly whipped double cream on to the bottom piece, cover with the scooped-out half (or whole if using smaller ones) of a passionfruit then set the top back on. Don't squish it down: you're after a jaunty, rakish angle. Proceed with the remaining five and set all six on a large plate, and let people help themselves as they want.

Serves 6.

When the two great Australian food writers, Stephanie Alexander and Maggie Beer, came to London some years back, I went to a dinner cooked by them; this was the pudding and I remain, all this time later, transfixed by it. Maggie Beer vaguely told me how she'd cooked them and I've hugged this information since then, longing to pass it on; this seemed the perfect opportunity.

It used to be that you could never lay your hands on a quince unless you had a tree, and so it was that the first thing I did when I bought a house with a garden was plant one, but now you can find them in Middle-Eastern stores pretty well off and on all year around, and in supermarkets for a few weeks from mid-August. Nothing matches their almost fantastically perfumed fragrance; and after this long, slow way of cooking them, their acid flesh turns to grainy, intense honeyedness, set to coral jelly at their centre, around the shiny black pips, the whole as darkly sticky as toffee apples. Serve these warm-to-room temperature, with a dollop of cold mascarpone on the side. Since cooking them takes almost 4 hours (though you are hardly involved) you're really going to have to start the dinner's pudding not long after you've cleared away lunch.

**1kg caster sugar**
**5 quinces**

**1 litre water**
**mascarpone or crème fraîche, to serve**

Put the sugar into a large, wide saucepan, cover with water, swirl to help the sugar start dissolving and add one of the quinces, cut up roughly. This is about the hardest thing you'll be doing here: it's a very simple recipe, but quinces are pretty well as solid as rock. Use a heavy, sharp knife and proceed with caution.

Bring quince, sugar and water to the boil and let boil away until you have a thick viscous syrup; this could take up to an hour.

Preheat the oven to 200°C/gas mark 6 and get out a roasting tin. Cut each of the remaining quinces in half, much as you would halve an avocado and put each one, cut side down in the tin. Pour over the syrup to come about 1cm deep and put the quinces into the oven for an hour. Turn the oven down to 160°C/gas mark 3 and cook for another 2–3 hours, basting (with the addition of more syrup if they're drying out) and turning regularly so that they caramelise and colour on both sides.

Remove from the oven and set aside, cut side up, so that the oven-scorched, red-glazed quinces stand in their sticky, ever-solidifying syrup as they cool. Set each half on a small plate, along with the mascarpone or crème fraîche, as you serve and eat with a teaspoon, dipping first into jellied, grainy flesh and then into the sharp, coolly contrasting cream on the side.

Serves 8.

# MINT JULEP PEACHES

There's something about mint juleps that I associate with the deep heat of midsummer. I have to say this association is an entirely literary one: I've never sat in the wilting sun drinking a mint julep in my life; the most I can muster is a few in cold college rooms in my cocktail-drinking student years (which certainly dates me). But there is, I always remember, I hope not erroneously, from *The Great Gatsby*, that pivotal scene, when they're all sitting around in the airless heat, deranged, before everything happens, drinking mint juleps. Anyway, there is something intensely summery – leafy, fresh, spicily aromatic – about these peaches, poached in sugar-syrup and bourbon and sprinkled with mint. Scotch whisky doesn't seem to have the mellow, rounded spiciness of bourbon, but if that's all you've got in the house . . .

| | |
|---|---|
| **700ml water** | **8 white-fleshed peaches** |
| **700g caster sugar** | **small bunch fresh mint** |
| **250ml bourbon** | |

Put the water, sugar and 200ml of the bourbon in a wide-bottomed saucepan, swirl about to help the sugar start dissolving a bit, and then put on the hob over medium heat and bring to the boil. Let it boil away for 5 minutes or so and then turn the heat down so that the syrup simmers; you want pronounced but not fierce bubbles. Cut the peaches in half and remove the stones and then lower these halves, so that they fit snugly, cut side down, in the pan (I find I get four to six halves at a time, depending on the pan I'm using) and poach for a couple of minutes before turning them over and poaching for another 2–3 minutes cut side up; obviously, the ripeness of the peaches will determine exactly how long they need cooking. (And if the peaches are very unripe, it will be much easier to remove the stones after cooking.) The best way of testing the peaches is to prod the cut sides with a fork; you'll be serving the fruit hump side up later and don't want any fork marks to mar the pink-cheeked beauty of these pale-fleshed peaches.

When they feel tender but not flabbily soft, remove with a slotted spoon to a dish and continue till you've cooked all the peaches. Pour the juices that have collected in the plate – pink from the colour of the skins – back into the poaching liquid, itself blush-deepened from cooking the fruit, then measure 200ml of the liquid into a small saucepan. Add the remaining 50ml of bourbon to this pan, put on the heat and boil till reduced by about half.

While this is happening, carefully peel off the skins; this should be easy enough. And on cooking, you'll see that the rosy fuzz leaves behind its markings on the white fruit, so that each peach half is tenderly coloured with an uneven pink.

You can leave the peach halves, cut side down, covered with clingfilm, on a plate till you need them. Should the peaches start turning brown on standing, just spritz with lime and their unsullied beauty will be restored.

Let the reduced syrup cool in a jug somewhere nearby; you can freeze the remaining poaching liquid to use the next time you want to make these (just top up with water and a dash or two of bourbon when you reheat). Before serving, pour some of the thick, pink-bronze syrup over the peaches and scatter the torn-off mint leaves, some left whole, some roughly chopped, on top.

Serves 6–8.

# WHITE CHOCOLATE ALMOND CAKE

This is one of those dense, pudding-suitable cakes, known in America as tortes, in which ground nuts are used in place of flour. I'm not sure that you would, unless told, detect the presence of the white chocolate, but its vanilla-scent butteriness lends itself beautifully to the delicate nuttiness of the ground almonds. This is a cake that looks plain, but its rich, eggy, marzipan texture makes it anything but. To taste this at its summery best, serve a roughly thrown together salad of mangoes, spritzed with lime, and maybe even dotted with raspberries, along with.

**175g white chocolate**
**150g soft unsalted butter**
**100g caster sugar**
**6 large eggs, separated**
**150g ground almonds**
**drop almond extract**

*to serve:*
**2 mangoes**
**juice of 1 lime**
**150g raspberries (optional)**

Preheat the oven to 180°C/gas mark 4. Grease and line a 23cm Springform tin; if you've got some almond oil to hand, use that, otherwise butter is of course fine.

Chop the chocolate and melt it in a bowl over a pan of simmering water or for a couple of minutes or so on medium in the microwave. Don't expect white chocolate ever to melt quite into the molten smoothness of dark: once it's lost its shape, it's melted enough; any more and it will start to seize. Put to one side while you get on with the cake.

Beat the butter until very soft, then add 50g of the sugar and cream again. Still beating, add the egg yolks one at a time, waiting till each one is incorporated before adding the next, then slowly scrape in the cooled, melted chocolate, beating firmly as you do so. Once the chocolate's smoothly incorporated, add the ground almonds and the almond extract, beating again to mix.

Whisk the egg whites till peaks begin to form, then slowly add the remaining 50g sugar until gleaming, glossy and firm.

Add a big dollop to the cake batter and stir well to lighten the mixture, then fold in the rest, gently, in three to four parts.

Pour into the prepared tin, and bake for 45–50 minutes or until cooked through. You shouldn't expect a plunged-in cake tester to come out exactly clean – this is, after all, a dense, damp sort of a cake – but no uncooked batter should be clinging to it. Anyway, when the cake's ready it should be beginning to come away from the sides of the tin. You should check the cake after about 30 minutes, though, as at this stage of cooking you'll probably need to cover the cake loosely with foil to stop it burning. Don't worry if it's caught slightly though: some bronzing at the top is a good thing.

Remove from the oven and sit the cake in its tin on a wire rack for about 20 minutes, before unspringing and inverting it, and letting it cool completely, though you can just as easily leave the cake in its tin, on the rack, to cool completely. This makes life much easier if you're transporting it, which – if you're picnic-bound, say – you might well want to.

Just before eating the cake, peel and chop up the mangoes roughly, wring out the mango skins over the fruit and add any mango juice that's collected while chopping. Add the raspberries if using, and squeeze in the juice of half the lime. Taste to see if you want the remaining half squeezed over, too. Toss well, but gently, to combine and serve alongside the richly contrasting cake.

Serves 8.

Don't think breakfast pancakes, but rather a dreamy, light, aromatic and sweet pudding, slicked with orange-flower syrup and nubbled with pistachios, to go after a vaguely Middle-Eastern dinner eaten languorously outside in the garden on a warm summer evening.

The syrup itself can be made in advance and just stored in a jar in the fridge, just as long as you remember to get it back to room temperature before you pour it over the cardamom-scented pancakes. If you forget, just fill a bowl or pan with hot water from the kettle and stand the jar in it until it returns to flowing form.

There is something about the yoghurt in the pancake batter that makes them incredibly light. As for the almond oil in them, you should find this easily in the super-market now, but if you can't, then use cooled, melted butter in its place. And you don't have to get busy at the stove at the very end of dinner to make these. Just cook them before you sit down at table, place them on a large baking sheet or ovenproof plate, tent with foil and keep them warm in a low oven (preheated to 120°C/gas mark ½) until you want to eat them.

**for the orange flower syrup:**
225g caster sugar
150ml water
juice of half a lemon
1 tablespoon orange-flower water

**for the pancakes:**
150g plain flour
1 tablespoon caster sugar
1 and a quarter teaspoons baking powder

quarter teaspoon bicarbonate of soda
pinch ground cardamom
3 tablespoons Greek yoghurt or labneh
approx. 125ml semi-skimmed milk
1 large egg
50ml almond oil (or 50g butter, melted and cooled)

**to serve:**
1–2 handfuls shelled pistachio nuts, chopped

To make the syrup, bring the sugar and water gradually to the boil in a saucepan, swilling the pan to help the sugar dissolve, but on no account stirring it. Once it's boiling, pour in the lemon juice and then turn down the heat a little and simmer the syrup for about 10-15 minutes until it coats the back of a spoon. Add the orange-flower water and simmer for another 5 minutes, then cool the syrup and chill in the fridge.

To make the pancakes, measure the dry ingredients into a large bowl then spoon the yoghurt into a measuring jug and, stirring with a fork, pour in the milk until you hit the 250ml mark. If you need to, add a little more than the 125ml specified to do so. Whisk in the egg and then the almond oil, then stir this jugful of wet ingredients into the bowlful of dry ones. Almost immediately the mixture will stiffen into a thick, fluffy batter.

Heat a dry griddle and when it is hot add about 2 tablespoons' worth of batter for each pancake. The mixture is quite thick, so you will need to encourage the pancakes into a round shape with the back of the spoon before the batter sets (they will be roughly 7cm in diameter). When the pancakes begin to bubble a little on top, flip them over and cook the other side to a golden brown.

Keep the pancakes warm under foil as you finish cooking the rest of the batter; you shouldn't need to sit them in the oven unless you're cooking these before dinner (see above).

When you are ready to eat them, and boy will you be ready, drizzle with cold syrup and sprinkle over a handful or so of ridiculously green, splintered and chopped pistachios.

Makes approximately 20; serves 8–10.

I call this blonde mocha simply because the chocolate, that is combined with the coffee to make this cake, is white rather than the usual dark – and because the name pleases me. If anything, though, the mixture works better than the traditional combination: the richness of the white chocolate offering an unfamiliar counterpart to the smoky depth of the coffee. It's not a light cake, I'll admit straight off, but that has never seemed to stand in its way. And although it's not what you might think of first off to serve on a summer's day, it's not just our haphazard climate that makes it all too often appropriate. There are, simply, times, whatever the weather, when you need something sweet with this amount of goo.

*for the cake:*
**225g self-raising flour**
**225g very soft unsalted butter,**
  **plus more for greasing tins**
**225g caster sugar**
**4 teaspoons instant espresso**
**4 large eggs**

**approx. 4 tablespoons full-fat milk**

*for the icing:*
**250g white chocolate**
**90g very soft unsalted butter**
**300ml crème fraîche**
**250g icing sugar, sieved**

Preheat the oven to 180°C/gas mark 4 and butter and flour two sandwich tins of 21cm diameter (and just under 5cm deep). But it's probably best, if it's at all warm out, to make the icing first and then stash it in the fridge till needed.

So: melt the chocolate and butter in a bowl over some simmering water or else in the microwave (but see note about melting white chocolate on page 214). Remove to cool a little, then add the crème fraîche – which you do need rather than ordinary cream, to undercut the otherwise oversweetness of the white chocolate – before gradually beating in the icing sugar. Put the icing in the fridge to set a little.

Now get on with making the cake. The easiest way is just to put the flour, butter, sugar, coffee and eggs in a processor and then, when fully incorporated, pour the milk – processing again after a little bowl-scraping with a rubber spatula – down the funnel to make for a soft, pouring consistency, adding more milk if needed but starting off just with a couple of tablespoons.

Remove the double-bladed knife, then pour and scrape the cake batter into the prepared tins and bake for 25 minutes or until a cake tester (or piece of raw spaghetti) comes out clean and the cakes are beginning to shrink away from the sides. Let them stand in their tins on a wire rack for 10 minutes then turn them out and leave them there till completely cool.

Now, cut out four strips of baking parchment and make a square with them on a cake-plate. Put one of the cakes on top, and add a good dollop of icing, spreading it almost, but not quite, to the sides and then cover with the remaining cake and spread the top and sides generously with the soft, rich, buttery icing. When it's all done, whip away the pieces of parchment, but not so roughly as to smear the icing over the plate, which would rather defeat the whole exercise.

Depending on the weather, you may want to put the assembled cake back in the fridge for 10 minutes or so before cutting.

Serves 8.

## SUMMER CRUMBLE

You could use any stone fruit you like here; I cannot resist an apricot. I love the thick-grained flesh, the way that dense-textured juiciness is so lusciously contained within the fruit's dappled, soft, baby-cheeked skin. This, I realise, is not how most apricots are when you buy them in the shops here, but cook them under a light layer of almondy crumble and disappointment can be averted: this pudding radiates mellow, good-mood sunniness.

**750g apricots, stoned and quartered lengthways**

**75g cold unsalted butter, cut into approx. 1cm dice**

**100g self-raising flour**

**25g ground almonds**

**75g caster sugar**

**50g flaked almonds**

Preheat the oven to 200°C/gas mark 6.

Put the apricots in a single layer in a shallow pudding dish.

Rub the butter into the flour and ground almonds, flutteringly working the pads of your thumbs and middle fingers until you have a mixture like rough sand. Stir in the sugar and flaked almonds and then sprinkle lightly over the apricots to cover them evenly.

Bake in the oven for about 30 minutes, by which time the crumble will have browned a little on the top and the fruit will be bubbling underneath. Serve with mascarpone or crème fraîche.

Serves 4–6.

# ICE CREAMS

I know everyone thinks that there's no point in making your own ice cream since you can buy such good stuff in the shops these days, but it just isn't true. First of all, I never quite buy into the usual worth-making/not-worth-making paradigm: nothing's worth making if the activity drives you to the edge of a nervous breakdown; anything can be rewarding if you actually get some pleasure out of the process. The strange thing about cooking is that obviously it is about an end product, and yet it isn't entirely.

Not that I've become an ice-cream maker out of a desire for the making of it alone. It's true I find mindless repetitive activity enormously relaxing (ie stirring a pan of custard for the ice cream's base) especially when stressed out, but I make ice cream because good home-made ice cream is nothing like the bought stuff. That dreamy, voluptuous texture, the subtlety of possible flavours – you just can't get any of that from a shop-bought tub, however expensive.

Making ice cream actually isn't difficult – it's all just stirring – but if you haven't got an ice-cream maker it is labour-intensive (which is a different matter). What you do then is put the cooled ice cream base into a covered container, stick it in the freezer and whip it out every hour for 3 hours as it freezes and give it a good beating, either with an electric whisk, by hand or in the processor. That gets rid of any ice crystals that form and that make the ice cream crunchy rather than smooth. If you've got an ice-cream maker, you're laughing: it then takes 20 minutes from having a cooled mixture to having an ice cream that's frozen but not set; it'll probably need another 20 minutes in the deep freeze for that. The important thing is, however you make it, once it's set hard, to let it ripen in the fridge for about 20 minutes before you eat it. You want it to be frozen, certainly, but not rock hard.

As for the method of making the custard for the ice cream, once you've got into the habit, it's – like everything else – routine. Just fill the sink half full with cold water for plunging the custard into if it looks like splitting at any stage.

Heat the specified amount of cream or milk till nearly boiling. Whisk the required yolks and sugar, and pour, still whisking, the warmed cream over. Transfer to a saucepan and cook till a velvety custard. I don't bother with a double boiler, and actually don't even keep the heat very low, but you will need to stir constantly, and if you think there's any trouble ahead, plunge the pan into the sink of cold water and whisk like mad. It shouldn't however take more than 10 minutes, this way, for the custard to cook. And when it has thickened, take it off the heat, add whatever needs adding according to recipe, then cool (I transfer the custard to a bowl and sit it in the cold water in the sink) before chilling and freezing in the ice-cream machine (or see manual tips above).

I know the list of ice creams below is a long one, but once you start, this ice-cream making thing becomes addictive, especially if you want to justify the extravagance of buying an ice-cream maker in the first place. Besides, you don't need summer as an excuse to make them – really you don't.

This is vanilla ice cream, but I just wanted to remind you that all it is is frozen custard, paired at its best with a bowl of warm, oven-poached rhubarb (following the rhubarb bit of the fool recipe on page 204).

**500ml full-fat milk**
**1 vanilla pod**
**6 egg yolks**

**125g caster sugar**
**150ml double cream**

Pour the milk into a saucepan. Cut the vanilla pod all down its length and, using the tip of the knife, scrape out the seeds into the milk in the pan. Now add the rest of the pod and bring almost to the boil. Turn off the heat, cover the pan and leave to steep for 20 minutes.

Whisk the yolks and sugar together, remove the pod from the milk and pour the milk into the eggy mixture, whisking as you go. Wash out the milk pan and pour the custard mixture back into the cleaned pan and heat, stirring, for 10 minutes or so until the mixture's thickened, following all the usual strictures on page 223. Let cool, stirring every now and again, then chill in the fridge. Just before freezing, whip the cream until thick, but not stiff, and fold it into the custard. Freeze as usual (see page 223).

Serves 6–8.

# APPLE ICE CREAM

The inspiration for this comes from Bella Radford, a contestant on *Masterchef* some years back now. It isn't her recipe, though on my request she did send it to me (which I characteristically and promptly lost) but *hommage* to it. I'd made a rhubarb ice cream for *How to Eat*, and just substituted the one fruit for the other. And in turn, if you want to try any other fruit ices, you can just use this as a blueprint. Eat as it purely, perfectly is, or turn it into an unfamiliarly elegant ice-cream sundae by piling it into a glass and topping with butterscotch sauce, which you make by melting 3 tablespoons of light muscovado sugar, 2 of caster sugar, 50g unsalted butter and 150g golden syrup in a pan over medium heat. When smooth, turn up the heat and let bubble away for 3–5 minutes. Then, off the heat, stir in 125ml single (or double) cream. Add some toasted flaked almonds on top for utter perfection.

**1kg cooking apples**
**100g caster sugar**
**300ml single cream**
**3 egg yolks**

**juice of 1 lemon**
**1 tablespoon Calvados (optional)**
**150ml double cream**

Peel, core and cut up the apples and put them in a pan with 50g of the sugar and cook till soft. Let cool and purée in a blender or processor then push through a sieve.

Make the ice cream as usual (see page 223) by heating the single cream, beating the remaining sugar with the yolks, whisking in the warm cream till a custard is formed, then adding the flavourings (lemon juice and Calvados, if using). Let cool.

Fold in the cold apple purée, whisk the double cream till thick but still soft and fold that in, too, and freeze as described on page 223.

# STRAWBERRY ICE CREAM

There is just something about home-made strawberry ice cream: it's the taste of blue skies, of sun on your shoulders; an idealised memory of summer in perfect culinary form. If you're up to it, and I don't mean by that anything much, as it's really pretty simple, make some vanilla shortbread (see page 207) to go with, but whatever, just make this: even using long-haul imported strawberries in bleakest February, it is sunshine-giving, life-transforming, sensational. (But first, do read page 223, for general ice cream tips.)

**500g strawberries**

**175g caster sugar, plus 2 tablespoons**

**500ml full-fat milk**

**500ml double cream**

**1 vanilla pod**

**10 egg yolks**

**2 tablespoons lemon juice**

Hull and roughly chop the strawberries, put them into a bowl and sprinkle over the 2 tablespoons of caster sugar and leave them to steep and infuse with flavour.

Pour the milk and cream into a heavy-based saucepan, and add the vanilla pod, split down the middle lengthways. Bring the pan nearly to the boil and then take it off the heat and leave to infuse for 20 minutes.

In a large bowl whisk the egg yolks and the 175g sugar until thick and pale yellow. Take the vanilla pod out of the milk and cream and pour, whisking the while, the warm liquid over the yolks. Put the cleaned-out pan back on the heat with the cream, milk, egg and sugar mixture and stir the custard until it thickens, then take it off the heat and pour it into a bowl to cool.

Purée the strawberries in a processor, and when the custard is cool fold in the lemon juice and strawberry purée.

At this point you can either freeze the ice cream in an ice-cream maker, or in a plastic tub in the freezer. If you do the latter you should remove it from the freezer after an hour and process it again, then put it back into the container for another hour before repeating the process, as usual (see page 223).

Serves 10–12.

Just as with ice cream, the glorious thing about home-made sorbet is that you can make flavours you could never buy in a shop. And the texture is so much better, too: smoother, richer, without all that icy brittleness. This sorbet is intentionally slushier still: a sluicing with Cointreau adds an orangey depth and keeps it all from freezing solid.

If you're not using an ice-cream maker, then just pour the sugary fruit purée into a plastic container and whip it out of the freezer and mush it up in a processor a couple of times while it freezes, following the instructions for machineless ice-cream making, on page 223.

**750g redcurrants**

**500g caster sugar**

**zest and juice of 1 orange**

**75ml Cointreau**

Preheat the oven to 180°C/gas mark 4. Put the redcurrants, stalks and all, into an oven-proof dish and add the sugar and zest and juice of the orange. Cover with foil and put in the oven for about 45 minutes, by which time the fruit will have become soft and pulpy.

Let the fruit cool before pushing the mixture through a mouli, or purée it in a blender or processor. The advantage of a food mill, though, is that it purées and sieves at the same time. A blended or blitzed mixture will have to be pushed through a sieve to remove all the pippy bits. Either way, make sure you use all the syrupy juice the redcurrants have made as well, and then stir in the Cointreau.

Put the sorbet mixture into an ice-cream maker to freeze and then decant this vivid puce slush into an airtight container and keep in the freezer until the actual point of serving.

Serves 6.

# PEACH ICE CREAM

This, again, is essence of summer, but you do need to use ripe, luscious, fleshy and sunny-scented fruit. Even so, I find that you get the best, most intense, flavour, from roasting the peaches first. If you're bowled over by the sheer, unimprovable peachiness of the fruit to hand you can ignore this step, but frankly, although it adds to the length of the whole procedure, sticking the fruit into the oven isn't exactly a difficult task, so I wouldn't make an issue out of it.

I am madly in love with crème de pêche (which is so much more peachy than, say, crème de cassis is redcurranty), and keep a bottle to hand to add to this ice cream, or to a glass of prosecco when the mood arises, but it's not an essential component.

**10 ripe yellow-fleshed peaches**
**6 tablespoons vanilla sugar or**
  **ordinary caster**
**juice of 1 lime**

**3 tablespoons crème de pêche (optional)**
**1 x 284ml tub single cream**
**4 egg yolks**
**1 x 284ml tub double cream**

Preheat the oven to 210°C/gas mark 7.

Halve the peaches, remove the stones, and sit them in a roasting tray, cut side up. Sprinkle half the sugar into the cavities, and then squeeze over the lime and roast for 20–30 minutes until softened and intensified in the heat.

Remove from the oven and leave to cool slightly before slipping the peaches out of their skins and into a food processor (a bit of skin left behind doesn't matter, however), making sure you catch every last bit of juice which you pour into the bowl of the processor, too, before blitzing to a purée. Transfer to a bowl, adding the crème de peche if you're using it, and leave to cool entirely while you get on with the custard.

So: in the usual way (see page 223), heat the single cream in a pan, beat the yolks and remaining sugar in a bowl and, while whisking, pour over the warmed cream. Make the custard in the normal way (page 223 again), and when it's completely cold, stir in the peach purée and then whip the double cream until thick and fold this in, too.

Freeze following all the usual instructions on page 223.

Top: left, Peach Ice Cream; right, Raspberry Ripple Ice Cream
Bottom: left, Baci Ice Cream; right, Gooseberry and Elderflower Ice Cream

Do not think of this in the same breath as the factory-made, whale-blubbered and artificially flavoured stuff. It's not even related. In fact, of all home-made ice creams, this is probably the most amazing: for the truth is, you cannot help but call to mind the vile (for most of us) original; this knocks you off your feet. It's like ice cream is meant to be, but so rarely is. It's what you want your childhood to have tasted of.

I should admit that the first time I made it, I got the ripple bit wrong (I tried to swirl it in for a minute in the machine rather than stippling by hand so all went pale pink and the definition was lost) but it still tasted like a reward for being placed on this earth.

If you don't want to fiddle about with the rippling, double the ingredients for the raspberry element, chill it in the fridge rather than freezing it and serve it dribbled over scoops of ice cream in bowls rather than veined through it. And trust me with the balsamic vinegar: it may not be traditional, but it really works.

**600ml single cream**
**6 egg yolks**
**200g caster sugar**
**1 teaspoon pure vanilla extract**

**125g raspberries**
**1 and a half teaspoons best-quality,**
   **syrupy balsamic vinegar**

Fill the sink half full with cold water in the normal, or that's to say, advised, way (see page 223).

Heat the cream till nearly boiling. Whisk the yolks and 150g of the sugar, and pour, still whisking, the warmed cream over. Transfer to a saucepan and cook till a velvety custard. When it has thickened, take it off the heat, add the vanilla, then cool before chilling and freezing in the ice-cream machine (or see manual tips on page 223).

While the ice cream's freezing, put the raspberries, remaining sugar and the balsamic vinegar in the processor and purée, then push through a nylon sieve to remove the pips (or just purée and depip at the same time by using a food mill). Then pour into a small, airtight container and stick it into the freezer to thicken but not to set hard.

When the ice cream's frozen, but not solid, put a third of it into a container and then dribble over a third of the semi-frozen, raspberry syrup, and repeat with another two layers of each. Take a wooden skewer and squiggle through so that the syrup ripples through the ice cream. Cover and put in the deep freeze till set.

Serves 6–8.

This is June in idealised gastro-form. Don't make me go on: words just cloud the issue. But know only that one mouthful of this, with its combination of tart fruit, floral syrup and egg-rich cream, makes you feel as you've been transported to a purer, better age. Eat and weep.

500g gooseberries

125ml elderflower cordial

2 tablespoons water

300ml single cream

100g caster sugar

3 egg yolks

300ml double cream, whipped

Put the gooseberries, elderflower cordial and water into a pan and cook, stirring every now and again, till the fruit has burst into mushiness. Take off the heat and when it's cooled down a little, purée either in a processor or blender, or just with a fork. Whatever: you don't want a super-smooth mixture here; a bit of texture is a good thing.

Make a custard in the normal way (see page 223): that's to say heat the single cream, beat the sugar and yolks, add the one to the other and put back on the heat, stirring, until thickened. Pour into a bowl and let cool. When the custard's completely cold, stir in the also-cold gooseberry and elderflower purée and then fold in the whipped cream. Freeze, observing all the usual strictures on page 223.

Serves 8.

Baci are those chocolate hazelnut kisses that I can't say are good, but are somehow compulsive, and you get this ice cream in every gelateria in Italy. Eat in cones, stuffed into brioches (see page 246) or simply in a bowl, with a sprinkling of chopped, toasted hazelnuts.

You can get the hazelnut syrup at any American coffee shop these days, and you do need it to get that intense, smoky, caramelly nuttiness.

Before you start, do read the ice cream tips on page 223.

**4 large egg yolks**
**100g caster sugar**
**500ml double or whipping cream**
**100g dark chocolate, minimum 70%**
   **cocoa solids**

**25g best-quality cocoa powder**
**1 x 200g pot Nutella**
**2 teaspoons hazelnut syrup**

Whisk the yolks and sugar in a bowl until thick and creamy; they should form pale ribbons when you lift the beaters or whisk. Bring the cream to the boil and add it to the beaten yolks, pouring slowly and beating all the while.

Melt the chocolate (I find this easiest to do in the microwave) then whisk this, followed by the cocoa, into the eggs and cream. Pour the chocolate-custard mixture into a pan and cook on a low to moderate heat, stirring constantly with a wooden spoon, until everything's smooth and amalgamated and beginning to thicken. Turn into a bowl or wide jug and cool, whisking or stirring every now and again to stop a skin from forming.

When the mixture's cool, whisk in the Nutella and the hazelnut syrup and then freeze in an ice-cream maker.

Serves 6–8.

# DIME BAR ICE CREAM

I used to have a really bad Dime Bar habit, which I cured by becoming a Dime Bar pusher. Now I'm just an occasional user. Still, this stuff is dangerously addictive . . .

**4 Dime Bars**
**600ml single cream**

**6 egg yolks**
**125g caster sugar**

Break the Dime Bars into pieces and put into a food processor and blitz till finely ground, like glassy sand. Tip out on to a plate and put in the fridge.

Warm the single cream. Whisk the yolks and sugar, then pour, still whisking, the warmed cream over the egg mixture. Transfer to a saucepan and cook till a velvety custard (see page 223). Cool then chill and, before pouring into the ice-cream machine, fold in the processer-pulverised Dime Bars.

Serves 8.

Do not be alarmed: no rarefied work or chocolate tempering is called for here. You just melt and mix and mould.

I have to admit that the inspiration for this comes from a rather low-rent variant: some entirely industrially made, chocolate-flavoured, vermicelli-coated balls, which I came across in a beach bar in Ibiza once. I prefer them dusted with cocoa rather than rolled in chocolate-flavoured sugar bits, but I am not trying to fashion them into elegant morsels, hence the inclusion of Bailey's.

Serve after dinner, with coffee, on hot summer evenings when a proper pudding feels like too much.

**150g dark chocolate, minimum 70% cocoa solids**
**200ml double cream**

**4 tablespoons Bailey's Irish Cream**
**5 tablespoons cocoa powder**

Break up the chocolate into small pieces and melt it with 100ml of the double cream in a saucepan, very gently.

Pour into a bowl, add the Bailey's and let the mixture cool. Then whisk the remaining 100ml double cream until soft peaks form, and fold it into the cooled chocolate mixture. Let it harden in the fridge for at least an hour or until you can shape it into balls.

Now do just that. It's messy work but not hard: take small nuggets into your hands and roll them into little balls, then dust them with cocoa (by rolling them into some cocoa sieved out on to a plate) and sit them on a Swiss roll tin which you simply place in the deep freeze. It's best not to make these in advance as their intense chocolatiness seems to fade after a couple of days in the freezer. And when you're serving them, don't take them out more than 10 minutes before you want to eat them: they need some of the raw chill taken off, but you don't want them to soften into unfrozen gunge.

Makes approximately 30.

# WHITE CHOCOLATE ICE CREAM WITH
# HOT BLACKBERRY SAUCE

The Ivy restaurant has a star-pudding on its menu which is a plateful of frozen berries with hot white chocolate sauce poured over them. It's immodest to say it, I know, but I prefer my version: the iced part is the white chocolate; the hot sauce, a tart, beaded river of blackberries. Scoop the ice cream into knickerbocker glory glasses, if you've got them, and pour the molten bramble sauce over. Even if you think you don't like white chocolate, you'll like this. (And before you start, do read the basic ice cream instructions on page 223.)

**for the white chocolate ice cream:**

| | |
|---|---|
| **500ml milk** | **50g caster sugar** |
| **4 egg yolks** | **200g white chocolate** |

Warm the milk. Whisk the yolks with the sugar, then pour – still whisking – the warmed milk over the egg mixture. Pour into a saucepan and cook till a velvety custard. Melt the white chocolate in the microwave – or in a bowl over a pan of boiling water – for 3 or so minutes, then whisk into the cooked custard. Cool, then chill then freeze in the ice-cream machine as normal (see page 223).

**for the sauce:**

| | |
|---|---|
| **1 punnet blackberries (approx. 150g)** | **1 teaspoon balsamic vinegar** |
| **4 scant tablespoons caster sugar** | **1 teaspoon arrowroot, slaked in a little** |
| **juice half a lemon** | **cold water** |

Put the berries, sugar, lemon juice, balsamic vinegar and 50ml water in a saucepan and bring to the boil, turn down heat and cook for a few minutes. Take the pan off the heat and stir in the arrowroot paste. Pour into a wide-mouthed jug or bowl with a ladle and take to the table with the ice cream.

    Serves 6.

# CHEESECAKE ICE CREAM

This started off as something of a culinary conceit: I wanted to recreate the flavour of cheesecake in ice-cream form. I don't claim it's an original idea – I'd once eaten cheesecake ice cream in a restaurant in LA, scooped into a lozenge-shaped ball and served alongside a mini blueberry pie – but striving for originality is frankly a grievous culinary crime. Never trust the sort of cooking that draws attention to the cook rather than to the food.

Anyway, this works exceptionally well, and is in some respects easier to make than regular cheesecake. I love to fold crushed digestive biscuits into the smooth, familiarly sharp-sweet mixture once it comes out of the ice-cream maker but isn't yet frozen solid, but you can leave the ice cream palely pure and sandwich it between two intact digestives as you eat.

| | |
|---|---|
| **175ml full-fat milk** | **1 egg** |
| **200g caster sugar** | **juice of half a lemon** |
| **125g Philadelphia cream cheese** | **350ml double cream** |
| **half teaspoon pure vanilla extract** | **50g digestive biscuits, crumbled (optional)** |

Heat the milk in a pan, and while it's getting warm, beat together the sugar, Philadelphia, vanilla and egg in a bowl. Still whisking, pour the hot milk into the cream cheese mixture and pour this back into the cleaned-out pan and make a custard in the regular way (see page 223).

Pour into a bowl and let it cool, at which time add the lemon juice and then the double cream, lightly whipped.

Freeze following the usual instructions on page 223, folding in the crushed digestives – if using – before the ice cream is set solid.

# MARGARITA ICE CREAM

This is surely what angels would eat at their hen night. I suppose it's the hopeful point of all cooking that the whole is greater than the sum of its parts, but never has this been more dreamily exemplified.

375ml double cream
6 large egg yolks
397g tin sweetened condensed milk
90ml tequila

30ml Triple Sec, Cointreau or even Grand Marnier, whatever you have to hand (I am permissive on this one)
juice of 6 limes and the zest of 1

Make a custard (see page 223) by heating the cream, whisking it into the egg yolks, and then pouring the mixture back into the cleaned-out pan, then cook it, stirring, until it's thickened. Pour it into a bowl and leave to cool a little, then stir in the condensed milk, tequila and Triple Sec (or Cointreau or Grand Marnier: I have used each of these in my time), lime juice and zest and then leave to cool completely before freezing in the normal way (see page 223 again).

For utter, unapologetic perfection, serve the ice cream in margarita glasses that you've first dipped in lime juice and then into a half-and-half, salt and sugar mixture. But just scooped into bowls, or on to cornets, this is hard to beat.

Serves 8.

# HONEY SEMIFREDDO

A semifreddo is not quite an ice cream, as the name – semi-cold, in translation – suggests. There's no custard to make, and no churning required as it freezes, which makes life very much easier. What you get is a smooth, soft block of chilled, almost frozen cream, with a texture of deep, deep velvetiness. This mellow, honey-flavoured version matches taste to texture. For some reason, sometimes when I make it, I end up with a block of uniformly buff cream; at others, I'm left with a honeyed, resin-coloured stripe along the base – or the top as it stands when you turn it out. But that's cooking for you. Either way, it works wonderfully. Pour more amber-coloured honey over as you serve, and scatter with toasted pine nuts, for quite the dreamiest, easiest pudding you could imagine.

**1 egg**

**4 egg yolks**

**100g best-quality honey, plus 3 tablespoons or so for serving**

**300ml double cream**

**25g pine nuts, toasted**

Line a 900g/1 litre loaf tin with clingfilm.

Beat the egg and egg yolks with the honey in a bowl, over a saucepan of gently simmering water, until the mixture is pale and thick. I use a wire balloon whisk for this, but if you feel like a bit of culinarily aided whirring, it will certainly be quicker with a hand-held electric whisk.

Whip the double cream until thick, and then gently fold in the egg and honey mixture. Pour into the prepared loaf tin, and cover carefully with clingfilm before putting it in the freezer for about 2–3 hours.

When it is ready to serve, turn out the semifreddo on to a suitably sized plate and drizzle this manilla-coloured log with honey, and sprinkle with the toasted pine nuts, before slicing. It thaws quickly as it stands, but that is part of its heavenly-textured charm. If you've got some dark, syrupy – indeed, honey-coloured – pudding wine to drink while you eat this, so much the better.

Serves 6–8.

# VIN SANTO ICE CREAM WITH CANTUCCINI

One of the loveliest puddings, if it quite counts as that, to order in restaurants in Tuscany, is a glass of vin santo, that resinous, intense, amber-coloured holy wine, with a few almond-studded biscuits to dunk in. The idea for this comes purely from that: the ice cream is further deepened by the addition of treacly muscovado sugar, and the wine in it keeps it voluptuously velvety, even after being frozen. You don't absolutely need to serve the cantuccini biscuits with it, but the combination is pretty well unbeatable.

**1 x 584ml tub double cream**
**200ml vin santo**
**8 egg yolks**

**6 tablespoons light muscovado sugar**
**1 packet cantuccini biscuits**

Heat the double cream in one pan, the vin santo in another. Whisk the yolks and muscovado sugar together and, still whisking, pour first the hot vin santo and then the warmed cream into them. Pour this mixture into a good-sized pan and make a custard as normal (see page 223). Allow to cool, then chill and freeze in an ice-cream maker or without, following the usual instructions on page 223. Serve by scooping out into small wine glasses, giving everyone some cantuccini to dip into the deep, almost incense-intense ice cream.

Serves 8–10.

There is a reason why this recipe is here. A year or so ago, in Sicily, I got up late one morning, went to a bar for breakfast and saw that instead of serving ice creams in cornets, they wodged a helping in the middle of a split, vaguely orange-scented brioche. I sat in the square, with a cup of coffee on the table, this exotic bun in my hand, having the best breakfast of my life.

Yes, I know that – especially in the heat of summer – making brioches at home is only one step away from madness, but you don't have to do this the purist way. Even if you don't feel like making everything from scratch, promise me the next time you invite people over for supper, you buy some little brioches from a proper pâtisserie and the best ice cream you can find, and serve them up, together, for the best pudding you will ever provide. Should you, however, feel like going in for a little domestic goddessery, then you need to have a blueprint to hand. I make the brioches much as I came across them in Sicily – that's to say, without their French, globe-topped, crenellated form – just shaped simply into slightly bulbous oblongs, their form a cross between a normal roll and a pain au chocolat. Round or rectangular, though, it doesn't matter: you just want them to provide a light, cakey casing for the ice cream that, burgerlike, they will later contain.

| | |
|---|---|
| **1 sachet easy-blend dried yeast** | **250g soft unsalted butter** |
| **50g caster sugar** | |
| **15g salt** | **for the glaze:** |
| **500g white bread flour, plus more for kneading** | **1 egg yolk** |
| | **orange juice** |
| **juice of half an orange** | **half a teaspoon of salt** |
| **6 eggs, beaten** | |

Put the yeast, sugar, salt and flour into a bowl, and add the orange juice and beaten eggs to mix to a dough. Using either a dough hook or your hands, knead until you obtain a smooth elastic mixture which will take about 10 minutes with a mixer or 20 minutes (sorry) by hand.

Cut the butter into small pieces and add them to the dough a little at a time, letting the dough absorb the butter in the mixer before you throw in the next piece. If you are doing this by hand then squeeze the butter into the dough gradually in the same way. Once the butter is absorbed keep kneading the dough until it is smooth, glossy and elastic.

Cover the bowl with clingfilm and leave it to double in size at room temperature; this will take about one and a half to two hours.

Knock back the risen dough by gently punching it to expel the air – which is one of the most gratifying things you will ever do in the kitchen – and then form it into a smooth ball putting it back into the bowl and covering again. Put the dough in the fridge for a couple of hours or ideally overnight, but don't leave it longer than 24 hours.

Before you are ready to cook the brioche buns, let the dough come to room temperature. When it is no longer cold, turn the dough on to a floured surface and knead again to make a large ball then pull off even-sized pieces to make about fourteen small rolls, shaping them into smooth rounds or ovals. You may want to make just about seven rolls and freeze the rest of the mixture as most of the ice-cream recipes above will not stretch to fill fourteen buns (but will certainly be enough for seven).

Put the shaped brioche buns on to baking sheets and glaze them with the beaten together egg yolk, orange juice and salt then leave to rise for about an hour until almost doubled in size. I know there is quite a bit of salt in the glaze but one of the wonderful things about these buns is the contrast between sweet and salt.

Meanwhile, preheat the oven to 200°C/gas mark 6.

Glaze again before baking and cook for about 15 minutes until the brioches are golden brown and sound hollow when you tap their bottoms. Leave to cool on a baking rack.

Makes about 14 buns.

# RED-HOT CHILLI SYRUP

Make this red-flecked, heat-infused syrup, leave to cool and pour over vanilla or chocolate ice cream (opinions are divided in my household over which provides the more fabulous combination) and feel the sun flare up inside you. OK, so it sounds odd, but the heat from the chilli is more of a peppery, spicy warmth than savoury kick. It's not that different from the sweet heat of crystallised ginger, come to think of it, which is itself glorious heaped over a pale mounding of vanilla ice cream.

**250g caster sugar**
**250ml water**

**1 long red fresh chilli, unseeded and very**
**finely chopped**

Put the sugar and water into a saucepan, and dissolve the sugar over a gentle heat. Then turn up the heat and bring to the boil and let bubble for 15 minutes or so until the liquid's reduced and you have a clear viscous syrup. When it's ready it should give the back of a wooden spoon a sticky glossy coating when you dip it in, but do not stir at any stage in the proceedings, or the syrup will crystallise.

Take off the heat and tip in the chilli, swirl (but again, do not stir) then pour into a glass jug to cool slightly, and then the syrup, now coral-tinted from the chilli, can be stirred so that the red flecks are distributed throughout, rather than just being suspended on the top.

You can keep this syrup in a tightly lidded glass jar till you need to use it. Should it set too hard, just stand the jar in a bowl of warm water to loosen up a little.

Makes enough for about 12 bowls of ice cream.

DRINKS

The traditional unit for cocktail mixing is a shot, which is equal to 25ml. If you haven't got a shot measure you could always use an old medicine cup, as unless you have some teeny-tiny measuring jugs it is hard to be accurate – not that accuracy is necessarily knife-edge here. Despite the precise quantities specified below, remember that this is really all a matter of taste.

Sugar syrups are available in specialist Off Licences, but if you can't track some down then make your own.

In a saucepan mix double the quantity of sugar to water over a low heat until the sugar melts. Then bring to the boil and simmer until you reach a syrupy consistency, remembering that the longer you simmer the thicker and stronger your syrup will get.

Allow to cool and then keep in the fridge; it will keep for a couple of months so it's worth making a big batch if you're in a cocktail-making groove.

*Previous page: Blue Lagoon*

## BLUE LAGOON

You need to have a certain determination of spirit to start mixing drinks with Blue Curaçao, but I've always found something liberating about having scant concern for good taste. This drink looks like the ocean – you just want to swim right into it – and is something of a citrussy killer.

**60ml (4 tablespoons) Blue Curaçao**       **7-Up**
**30ml (2 tablespoons) vodka**       **lime juice**

Pour the Blue Curaçao and vodka into a glass, fill up with 7-Up and add a spritz of lime juice. Shut your eyes and knock it back.
      Makes 1.

## PINA COLADA

I think this is what's known in the trade as a classic cocktail. Others may sneer. Let them. And if you're too embarrassed to stand at a bar and order one, stick Barry Manilow on the turntable and pour freely at home. Cocktail umbrella optional.

**100ml white, dark rum or Malibu**       **50ml coconut cream**
**100ml pineapple juice**       **handful of ice cubes**

Put the ingredients into a blender and whizz on the cocktail-shaker button till smooth. Pour into a tall glass.
      Makes 1.

## ELDERFLOWER AND PASSIONFRUIT COOLER

This is the perfect drink to have by the pitcherful for summer lunches in the garden: easy to make, easier still to drink.

**elderflower cordial**　　　　　　**ice cubes**
**fizzy water**　　　　　　　　　　**sprigs fresh mint**
**3–4 passionfruit (strained if preferred)**

In a large glass jug, pour about one-third elderflower cordial to two-thirds fizzy water. Add the pulp and seeds of the passionfruit (or strain them if you prefer this pipless) and then chunk up with ice cubes, adding a few sprigs of fresh mint if you have any to hand.

　　　Serves 6.

## MINT AND LIME COOL AID

This is the perfect, sweet-sharp drink, like lemonade only more so, for a hot summer's day. There's nothing to stop you adding a slug of vodka, but I love this as it is, in its pure, unalcoholic state.

**8 limes (or enough to make 250ml juice)**　**1.25 litres water**
**200g caster sugar**　　　　　　　　　　**ice cubes**
**bunch fresh mint, some sprigs**
**  reserved for the jug later**

Remove the zest of 4 of the limes using a vegetable peeler and put this, along with the sugar, mint and 250ml of the water into a saucepan and bring to a boil, stirring to dissolve the sugar. Once it's started boiling, turn the heat down and let the liquid simmer in the pan for about 5 minutes. Take off the heat, let cool and then strain into a jug.

　　　Squeeze the limes to make about 250ml juice and then add, along with the rest of the water to the jug of syrup. Add ice cubes and a few sprigs of mint.

　　　Serves 6–8.

Left: Mint and Lime Cool Aid; right: Elderflower and Passionfruit Cooler

## GINGER BEER SHANDY

Purists will insist you use bitter for this, but I am too much of a girl, and like it best made with fizzy foreign lager. For that real, deck-chair bound summer feeling, drink in a reclining position, with a bulging sandwich – filling immaterial; white bread obligatory – clamped in your glass-free hand.

**1 small bottle of fridge-cold lager**  **1 fridge-cold can of ginger beer**

Pour the lager into a tall glass and then top up with as much ginger beer as you like.
Makes 1.

## GINA

I don't know where this originates or why it is so named, but I like to think it is in honour of La Lolla. The classic version uses gin; I prefer the clearer, less old-lady hit of vodka. And don't be confined by the suggestion of crème de cassis: use any alcoholic fruit syrup you like. I often make a light and floral Peach Gina by substituting a slosh of crème de pêche de vigne (and see page 231) instead.

**50ml crème de cassis**  **1 tablespoon lemon juice**
**25ml vodka**  **approx. 200ml fizzy water**

Pour the first three ingredients over ice and then top up with fizzy water in a tall glass.
Makes 1.

# TOM COLLINS

A Tom Collins is a Tom Collins because the original, authentic key ingredient was a couple of shots of Old Tom gin. But this is not worth making an issue of. You could try and track it down, but I never have: just use whatever gin you have in the house instead. For me that's Plymouth gin, but I don't think it pays to be too rarefied about such specifications here. For me the crucial factor is all that lemony fizz, no matter how exactly you choose to spike it. And if you haven't got sugar syrup, just spoon a tablespoonful of caster sugar into the measured out lemon juice and let both stand for 10 minutes or so until the acid's dissolved the sugar before mixing into the rest of the drink.

**50ml gin**
**25ml lemon juice**

**1 tablespoon sugar syrup**
**soda or fizzy mineral water**

Pour the first three ingredients into a tall glass over ice, and top up with fizzy water.
Makes 1.

# LEMON DROP

This is citron pressé for grown-ups: frosty-white, acid sharp and as deeply lemony as you could want.

**1 lemon, peeled (and see page 96 for precise instructions if you feel it necessary) and quartered**
**1 tablespoon caster sugar (or sugar syrup)**

**50ml limoncello or other lemon liqueur**
**50ml Triple Sec**
**handful of ice cubes**

Put the lemon pieces into the goblet of a blender, sprinkle over the sugar and leave to steep to let the sugar dissolve for a few minutes (if you're using sugar syrup, just bung it all in, everything you've got, and blitz away) then pour in the limoncello and Triple Sec, tumble in the ice cubes and whizz away on the cocktail-shaker setting or however your blender is organised. When everything's combined, thickened and ice-white, pour into a large tumbler and knock back.
Makes 1.

# PASSIONE

I don't know why, when I make cocktails, I start worrying about the particular quality of the individual ingredients, but I like to use Plymouth gin here. Certainly, its flavour is better – more delicately aromatic – than any other gin's, but I won't kid you that this is immediately detectable in this heady concoction.

**60ml (4 tablespoons) gin**　　　　　　**lime juice**
**60ml (4 tablespoons) Southern Comfort**　**handful ice cubes**
**juice of 2 large passionfruit, sieved**

Pour gin and Southern Comfort into a large beaker, and add the passionfruit juice and a spritz of lime. Add ice, up-end another beaker on top of the glass (or use a cocktail shaker to start off with) and shake to mix, then strain into a waiting martini or daiquiri glass.

Makes 1.

# JOURNALIST

I found a version of this in *Ben Reed's Cool Cocktails* and couldn't resist. Its name tells you everything you need to know: boozy, acerbic and packing quite a punch, this is a drink with lethal edge.

**25ml gin**                                              **1 tablespoon lemon juice**
**1 teaspoon sweet white vermouth**        **1 and a half tablespoons Triple Sec**
**1 teaspoon dry vermouth (also white)**    **few drops Angostura bitters**

Shake everything above in a cocktail shaker over ice, then strain into a martini glass. Drink and get straight to your Remington.

     Makes 1.


# POMME POMME

Yes, it's a ludicrous name, but I couldn't help myself. And anyway, this is perfect poured out of chilled jugs over a long, hot summer.

**1 litre carton apple juice**                    **15 tablespoons/225ml apple schnapps**

Pour both juice and liqueur into a jug and throw in a handful of ice cubes.

     To make a single glassful, just measure out 3 tablespoons of apple schnapps into a glass, toss in some ice cubes and pour over 200ml of apple juice. You should also know that this is very good – though strictly speaking requires a different name – made with Triple Sec and orange juice. Feel free to add a few slices of orange into the jug, too.

     Serves 6.

# PIMMS

This is English summer in liquid form. Spicy, mellow, light and refreshing, this is a reminder that in matters of food and drink, originality and innovation are so not the point.

**200ml Pimms**
**600ml lemonade**
**half a cucumber, sliced**
**half an orange, sliced**
**half a lemon, sliced**

**1 small apple, cored and sliced**
**small bunch fresh mint**
**a few borage flowers, should you have them growing in your garden**
**handful fresh strawberries, hulled and halved**

Mix everything together in a big jug and throw in a handful of ice. Or better make that two jugs: this is not something that anyone ever has just one glass of.

Serves 6.

# CAMPARI SODA

Oh please, I know this is not something that requires a recipe – perhaps merely a reminder. When I think of summer, I think of this. I drink it, however, all the year round.

**100ml Campari**

**200ml soda water or to taste**

Pour the ingredients into a glass over ice and add a slice of orange.

Makes 1.

# FRAGONARD

Think Bellini, only with puréed strawberries in place of peaches: it's the taste of lyrical, wide-skied summer. In actual fact – which I found out long after its inception in my hands – this is known in Italy as a Rossini, but I stick stubbornly to the particular connotations of my naming.

**1 bottle prosecco (or other fizzy white wine)**

*for the purée:*
**500g strawberries (hulled)**
**2 tablespoons crème de fraise (optional)**

For 1 bottle of prosecco (or other fizzy white wine of your choice) add a purée made (in the blender or food mill) from 500g hulled strawberries and, if you can get some, a couple of tablespoons of crème de fraise. If you haven't got any crème de fraise, that sweetly alcoholic essence of strawberry, and the fruit you're using is not truly red 'n' ripe, then you may need to add a spoonful or so of sugar while blitzing. Stir well and pour; I find I get about seven assorted glasses' worth out of the above quantities.

Serves 6.

## FRESH GREEN GIMLET

This takes inspiration in part from a mojito, that bar classic of the late nineties – mint, sugar syrup, lime, rum and soda – and in part from a gimlet, that intense and trad mix of vodka and lime cordial. And frankly, this child outstrips either of its parents. When I gave it to a friend to taste after making it for the first time, I had to fight to get the glass back from her.

**1 tablespoon caster sugar**
**juice of 1 lime**
**small handful of fresh mint leaves**

**50ml vodka**
**a fistful of ice cubes or crushed ice**
**dash of fizzy mineral water (or to taste)**

Spoon the sugar into a large tumbler, squeeze over the lime juice and stir to dissolve. Add the mint leaves and stab away at them in the tumbler with the end of a rolling pin; this is what's known in the business as 'muddling'. Add the vodka and ice, swill to mix and then top up with the dash of fizzy water.

Makes 1.

## ALCOHOLIC ICED COFFEE

My father told me that I had to include a recipe for iced coffee here, and of course he's right. He meant by this, a tall glass of cold, cold milk dappled with Camp, and I quite see his point. But I find I move more and more towards the Italian *caffe freddo*: a viscous, black shot of espresso, a copious amount of sugar added to the pot while still hot, to which you can add milk as you wish on serving. Better still, turn it into a *shakkerato* by whizzing it up when cold with a handful of ice cubes in the blender to make a milk-less but creamy-topped glass of liquid black velvet. This is an alternative, after-dinner version and all too *potabile*.

**1 tablespoon coffee liqueur**
**50ml chilled espresso coffee**

**sugar syrup or caster sugar to taste**

Mix all the ingredients together and pour into a shot glass. Or, if it's easier, add sugar to taste when you make the espresso and then just mix with the coffee liqueur when it's cold; this way you don't need to bother with making or getting hold of any sugar syrup. If it's a real morning-after wake-up call you need, add a shot of vodka as you mix.

Makes 1.

# SANGRIA

This is party-time, Spanish-style. And like all drinks that become debased through popular consumption, it is much better than snobbish instinct would lead you to believe.

**1.5 litres red wine – a good, fruity
 Cabernet Sauvignon if you can**
**200g caster sugar**
**50–75ml brandy, to taste**

**1 lemon, sliced**
**1 orange, sliced**
**1 apple, cored and sliced**
**fizzy water**

Mix everything together, except the fizzy water, and using the smaller quantity of brandy, in a large jug and let it macerate overnight in the fridge.

Taste and add more brandy and sugar if necessary, it should taste fairly strong and syrupy. Then mellow the drink with some fizzy water until it has the consistency of wine, add ice to chill but not so much as to dilute it. To be entirely proper, this should be ladled into glasses out of a large bowl, but I don't think we need to be too fanatical on this point. Even I admit there is such a thing as going too far.

Serves 6.

# KIWITINI

There's something about the intense, sour fruitiness of this, as well as its beautifully black-speckled, lusciously thick greenness, that induces a feeling of summery well-being. The kiwi had its moment in cuisine many years ago, and has since been a cipher for culinary silliness, but in drinks it has a serious argument to make. Part smoothie, part martini, pure heaven: and you are only a blender-moment away.

**25ml chilled vodka**
**50ml chilled dry martini**

**1 peeled kiwi**

Put the above ingredients in a blender (with a handful of crushed ice if you so wish) and blitz to a cool, velvety purée. Pour into a martini glass and enjoy.

Makes 1.

# MOSCOW MULE

The hot kick of ginger beer is peculiarly desirable in the heights of summer. If you want to wallow a little more intensely in the experience, then grate in – with a microplane, ideally – a little fresh ginger for a more heady pep.

**45ml (3 tablespoons) vodka**
**juice of half a lime**

**fresh ginger, finely grated**
**ginger beer, ice cold**

Pour the vodka into a glass, add the lime juice and, if you've got some around, some fresh, finely grated ginger, and then fill up the glass with ice-cold ginger beer.

Makes 1.

Opposite: Kiwitini

When I was an undergraduate in the Brideshead (that's to say Re-Revisited) Era of 1980s Oxford this was the drink of choice at many a pretentious cocktail party. It's not a cheap way to get drunk, but remember we're talking the age of the *jeunesse dorée* here: I seem to remember sipping this under a veiled pillbox hat, the ash from a Sobranie Black Russian flicked from a mesh gloved finger tip. I feel better for getting this off my chest now.

Ideally, this should be shaken over ice, so as not to dilute it, but if you're making a jugful (and basically, it's just one third of each ingredient, sugar syrup to taste) it makes life easier if you just toss a handful or so of ice cubes in with it.

**25ml Plymouth (or other) gin**
**25ml Cointreau**
**25ml lemon juice (about half a lemon's worth)**

**1 tablespoon sugar syrup (or dissolve a tablespoon of caster sugar in the lemon juice first)**
**ice cubes**

Shake the ingredients over ice and pour into a glass.
Makes 1.

# INDEX